# What
Can
| Say?

# What Can I Say?

## SHEILA DAINOW

PIATKUS

Copyright © 1999 Sheila Dainow
First published in 1999 by
Judy Piatkus (Publishers) Ltd
5 Windmill Street, London W1P 1HF

**The moral right of the author has been asserted**

*A catalogue record for this book is available from the British Library*

ISBN 0–7499–1951–5

Designed by Sue Ryall

Typeset by Phoenix Photosetting, Chatham, Kent
Printed and bound in Great Britain by
Mackays of Chatham PLC, Chatham, Kent

# DEDICATION

*During the course of writing this book, one of my daughters faced a life-threatening condition. This book is dedicated to Jo and all those friends and family who supported us by knowing exactly what to say.*

# Contents

# ACKNOWLEDGEMENTS

This is an opportunity to thank all those people who spoke to me about their experiences and allowed me to quote them. Thanks, too, to Carole Blake for her ever-present support and to all at Piatkus for their patience and help. As always, I am indebted to Cyl, who is still providing tea, sympathy and computer therapy!

# INTRODUCTION

Have you ever been in a situation when words failed you? Someone you care about has told you something which shocks or upsets you so much you can't think how to respond. A friend tells you he or she is gravely ill; a colleague confides in you about depression; someone in your family is seeking divorce. You want to say and do the right thing, but your mind has gone blank. This book is about such occasions and aims to help you respond as helpfully as possible.

It is natural to want to help the people we care about when we hear they are in trouble, but it can be difficult if we are afraid of saying the wrong thing or doing something which might make matters worse. On the other hand, when we have a problem we look to our nearest and dearest for support, practical and emotional.

Part 1 of the book goes through some of the reasons why it can be so hard to help, and offers some general ideas for good communication. For instance, it looks at the different ways in which it is possible to listen and talk, and how some of these are better than others in difficult situations.

Part 2 focuses on some particular situations such as illness, redundancy and death. It offers practical advice for managing those occasions when it is often difficult to know what to say for the best. Each chapter includes some general ideas about what is happening to people and why they may be responding the way they are, and specific suggestions on helpful things to do and say. The quotes are from people who were willing to talk about their own experiences as I was writing the book. Although everyone's experience is different and personal to them, it is sometimes comforting to know that other people have gone through and survived similar problems.

This is a book to use as and when you need it; but you might want to read it through to get a sense of how good communication can contribute to your ability to comfort, support and help others in need. However, you don't have to read it from beginning to end like a novel – you can browse through it and pick out the parts that seem most relevant at the time. It is a useful book to keep on a handy shelf for reference when you just don't know what to do. It can help you to find the right words for the occasion, whether you want to comfort someone who is upset or help someone to express their anger; make a critical comment without causing a row; respond to bad news or motivate someone to action.

# PART 1

# 1

# SETTING THE SCENE

There is nothing more frustrating than wanting to give someone comfort or help and just not being able to say what you are
feeling and thinking. What words can you use, for instance, to
someone who has just lost someone very close to them? How can
you show your sympathy to parents who have just discovered
their baby is disabled? What about supporting a person who has
just lost their job? Many of us do find it difficult to know what
to say or do, even though we want to help as much as possible.
As with many problems, there isn't a simple solution. Several
factors affect the way we respond to others in such situations,
and this chapter sets the scene by looking at some of them.

## *Fight Or Flight*

It might surprise you, even shock you, to think of yourself as
self-interested – after all, you are reading this book because you

want to be of help to others. However, each of us is affected by self-interest. This is not the same thing as selfishness, which is the gratification of our own needs at the expense of anyone who might stand in our way. Self-interest is our natural and necessary constant monitoring of our situation in order to maintain our safety and survival. Sometimes we are very conscious of how our senses are checking the environment to identify any possible threat to our safety, but most of the time this process goes on outside our awareness.

To understand why we do this, we need to go back to the time when humans were evolving. Just for a moment, pretend you are one of your earliest ancestors, perhaps living in the Stone Age. There you are, gathered with your family in your cave, munching on a bit of mammoth, when the shadow of an enormous creature falls across the wall at the back of the cave. The sabre-toothed tigers are on the prowl! What can you do? Well, basically you only have two options. You can stay and fight, or run away. The threat is a matter of life and death, so you don't have much time to make the decision. The mechanism which developed to get us out of that kind of trouble is still part of our make-up today. The process is triggered by information delivered to the brain from our senses, which are constantly monitoring the environment. As soon as any threat to our survival is detected, our body is alerted to the need for action. A chain of events starts in our central nervous system to equip us with what we need in order to fight the threat or flee from it.

This is a problem because, although it was a brilliant way of dealing with the physical threats that our ancestors faced in prehistoric times, the kind of threats that we face in modern life are not *always* of a simple physical nature. For instance, our own sense of safety can be shaken by what happens to others. Another person's bereavement warns us of our own mortality;

someone else's misfortune can cause us to feel apprehensive about our own future or guilty at our continuing good luck. But hearing this kind of information can have the same physiological effect on us as our ancestors experienced when they saw the shadow of the tiger.

Our body and mind respond automatically to what seems like a threat to our own equilibrium. Can you remember how you responded the last time you heard some distressing news from someone close to you? Obviously everyone is different, and the effect on you personally would have depended on individual factors, but you probably experienced a physical reaction: your breathing rate may have quickened, you may have become aware of the speeding of your heart, sweating in your palms, a strange feeling in the pit of your stomach.

All these feelings are signs that the 'fight/flight' response has been triggered. What we are programmed to do, of course, is to overcome or get away from the 'threat'. In fact, you might remember that the first thing you wanted to do was run away or deny that anything untoward was happening.

This kind of instinctive response makes it difficult to communicate, because so much of our energy is being used in controlling our reaction. We can feel confused and worried about doing the wrong thing. Our embarrassment can make us literally speechless or pointlessly glib. Understanding this process means we can acknowledge the effect and take steps to calm ourselves, perhaps just taking a deep breath before speaking, so that we can respond in the most helpful way.

## *Controlling Our Critic*

Fear can have a paralysing effect. What kind of fears leave us tongue-tied? Saying the wrong thing; appearing clumsy, insensitive or uncaring; giving way to our own feelings, or appearing patronising might appear on your list. In the cold light of day it is easy to see how silly these fears are. It is generally true to say that other people are not carefully monitoring our responses, matching them against their idea of what is right. When people are in trouble, they are much more likely to be hurt by being ignored, discounted or even isolated than by a misplaced word or gesture. But when we are actually faced with the reality of someone's grief, anger or confusion, our fears can overwhelm us.

One way of looking at this is to imagine we have a critic following us around and constantly judging us, apparently expecting us to make a mistake. Every time we consider saying or doing something the familiar internal voice will make itself heard: 'If you say that, you'll look stupid'; 'You shouldn't do anything – you'll only make things worse'; 'What makes you think you're important enough to help?' and so on. If you recognise this voice, learn to talk back. The idea of talking back to yourself may seem odd, but it is worth trying if you want to refute and reject those habitual ways of thinking which get in our way.

## Switching off

There are several ways of doing this. You can confront this inner voice directly by thinking about what you might say to a real person who was dogging you in this way. Think of a phrase which would help you counter what you are hearing, for example:

- I have a right to say what I feel
- You can't stop me
- I know I can help
- Be quiet and let me get on with it

If you are wondering where this critical voice comes from, it is likely that it developed fairly early in your life. During your childhood your parents, or those people who brought you up, taught you how to behave, how to keep safe, what was right and wrong and so on. You probably experienced them praising, rewarding and loving you when you were good and punishing you when you did something wrong or dangerous. These punishments, physical or verbal, signalled withdrawal of our parents' approval, and so were very powerful.

Such control mechanisms remain in our conscious or unconscious memory and can emerge as our internal critic whose task it is to keep us on the right road. You may even find that the voice you hear so clearly in your head is amazingly similar to that of your actual mother or father, or whoever it was who disciplined you in those early years.

Another way to switch off the critic voice is to ask yourself the cost of obeying it. Avril, for instance, felt very nervous about contacting a recently bereaved friend. She was afraid of making her more upset by saying the wrong thing or intruding on what should be a private time. She thought about the possible costs of following this line and came up with this list:

- Her friend would think she didn't care
- She wouldn't have an opportunity to share thoughts and feelings
- As time passed, it would be more difficult to initiate contact
- Eventually losing contact altogether

Listed like this, it seemed a very high price for Avril to pay. She gave her critic a talking-to and decided to take the risk.

## You are worth the risk

Probably the best way of dealing with this whole problem is to realise that you are worth as much as anyone else. You know that you are trying to do the best you can in managing the business of living, and that you are as worthwhile as every other person who is trying to do the same thing. Once you can truly believe this of yourself, you will trust yourself to behave naturally and appropriately whatever the situation. It won't be so necessary for you to do the right thing – whatever that is. You won't need to fear failure or rejection.

Of course, you might make mistakes – every human being does. However, mistakes are just mistakes; if you make one you can apologise or change your behaviour. A mistake does not make you a bad person – you are just someone who with hindsight would have done something else.

## *Guilt: A Useless Emotion*

Another factor that can play a role in the quality of our contact with others is guilt. It is a feeling that we are bad for doing what we are doing, because the action is contrary to our image of how we feel we are expected to behave. It is very natural to feel distress, regret, sadness and concern on hearing about someone else's problem; these are feelings which usually lead to supporting and helpful action. What is less helpful is to feel guilty that you don't have the same problem, and then allow that feeling to stop you going out to the person in the belief that they will blame or resent you.

If you have had a painful experience which changed your perspective on life altogether, you will know just how shocking it can be. You probably experienced a mixture of emotions, including anger and resentment at the unfairness of life. You may well have directed these feelings towards people who seemed to be free of problems. You might even have harboured thoughts about other people who you felt deserved your problem more than you. This projection of painful feelings on to someone else is one of the ways we try to deal with them.

It can feel hurtful if you are the person on whom the feelings are being projected – but you need to understand that it isn't really personal. These feelings aren't about you; rather, they are an indication of the depth of the pain the other person is experiencing. It is as if they can lighten their burden by transferring some of it on to someone else. Of course, the relief is only momentary; blaming or resenting someone else doesn't change the situation at all.

If you find yourself with guilt feelings which are stopping you approaching someone, probably the best way of dealing with them is to share them with the person involved. It can be extraordinarily therapeutic to be able to talk about thoughts and feelings which you might feel ashamed at having. The talking doesn't solve the original problem, but it can open the way to a deeper, truer kind of communication which can be most helpful for both of you.

Chapter 2 explores the possibilities for such communication.

# 2

# CAN YOU HEAR ME?

Good communication rests on understanding and being understood. It wouldn't really matter how clever and articulate we were if no one understood the message we were trying to get across. This chapter explores how to listen in order to understand as much as possible.

Can you remember the last time you were in a room with a lot of people talking to each other? Perhaps it was a party with groups of people all talking together, or it could have been a business meeting or a conference, a family gathering or a dinner party with friends. If you had stood back for a while and watched what was happening you might have noticed that, although a lot of people were talking, not everyone was listening. One person, for instance, might have been describing their latest holiday, another criticising the latest government policy announcement, someone else talking about their problems at work and so on.

While the talk is going on you might notice some listeners

begin to fidget, their eyes start to wander. What is likely to be happening is that they are rehearsing their response, listening more intently to the voice in their own head than to the person speaking. The deal seems to be, 'I'll give you space to say what you want and then you have to be an audience for me.' The event seems like a success because people are apparently communicating, but many will go home without having been properly heard or having really listened to others.

Listening is a crucial skill for making and maintaining relationships. Good listeners draw people to them. Their friendships are deep and lasting; people feel comfortable with them and want to share their thoughts and feelings. The good listener seems to understand what you are trying to communicate even if you don't feel very articulate. Think for a moment of someone you know is a good listener and see if you can identify what it is that they do and how you respond.

On the other hand, people who don't listen are not as rewarding to be with; they seem to be more interested in themselves than in anyone else. When you are with them, you get the feeling that you are there to provide an audience for them rather than to join together in a conversation. If you know someone who you feel is a bad listener, think about what they do and how you respond to them.

Listening is particularly crucial when you are with someone who really does want or need your help or support. This probably sounds obvious, but the problem is that listening is not as easy as it may seem. Although we do it all the time, it is something of which we are not particularly conscious. It just happens.

However, there is more to it than that. Good listening is an active process which needs you to do more than just be there and stay quiet. Remember that communication is the art of

understanding and being understood. In order to understand
the other person you might need to ask questions, check your
understanding, summarise what has been said, maybe even
challenge in order to encourage the person to explore their
thoughts. You could think of yourself as an active associate in
the process of communication, rather than a passive partner.
Here are some ways you might go about this:

## Use Your Own Words

This means rephrasing what you think someone has just said,
putting it into your own words. Paraphrasing like this is a
useful discipline in any situation where communication is
important, because it keeps you trying to understand what the
other person means. When someone tells you something, you
can respond with a phrase like 'In other words . . .'; 'So you are
saying . . .'; 'What I think you are saying is . . .'; 'So you were
feeling . . .'; 'Do you mean . . .?'; 'Let me see if I understand
what you mean . . .', following with what you have heard.

This simple, basic skill can reap tremendous rewards. It is a
very good way of cooling down an angry exchange. You are less
likely to misunderstand the situation or make false assumptions
or come over as judgemental, aggressive or dominating. You
are more likely to remember what was said. And perhaps more
important than any of these, the other person will feel heard
and realise you are committed to trying to understand them.

## Ask Questions

You need to clarify a few things to get the full picture. Perhaps
you want to ask for more facts or background information; to

know something of the context and maybe the relevant history. You will want to know how the person thought and felt, or how they are reacting now. The obvious way to get this information is to ask questions.

## The wrong kind

However, even that isn't as simple as it might seem. Some questions have the effect of turning off a conversation rather than paving the way for continued contact. For example, it's very common to start off a question with the word 'Why?' Sometimes, though, this 'why' can have a strange effect. People can feel grilled, interrogated, defensive, criticised – even though the questioner has none of these intentions. Maybe it's because it's a question which, particularly when we were children, was often preceded by a judgement or criticism, and we got used to having to defend or justify ourselves. Whatever the reason, people often respond defensively and experience the questioner as being without sympathy or understanding.

While we are on the subject of unhelpful questions there are a couple more examples worth exploring. It's possible to ask a question as a way of masking a criticism or judgement. These are the kind of questions to which the answer you are looking for is obvious! 'Don't you think it would be better if you . . .' is a good example. Whatever comes next is the questioner's opinion of what the person should be doing – so they have to answer either 'Yes' to please or placate the questioner, or 'No' and have an argument. Either way, the communication is potentially contaminated.

Another type of question to avoid if you are aiming for an easy communication climate are ones which can be answered with the words 'Yes', 'No' or 'Don't know'. These are called closed questions, because they tend to close off the conversation. For example, 'Do you feel angry?', 'Are you going out today?' You can easily get into a situation where you are asking these kind of questions, the other person answers 'Yes' or 'No', leaving you to carry on the conversation, so you ask another question and the whole scene begins to feel like an interrogation.

## The right kind

What you want to do is concentrate, as far as possible, on asking questions which invite the other person to go on talking. These usually begin with phrases like 'How are you feeling about . . .', 'What happened?', 'What do you think about . . .?', 'What would you like me to do?' You can probably see how these questions are opening a door rather than closing it. Obviously, though, there will be times when you need to ask a simple question: 'How do you feel about what time it is?' instead of 'What's the time?' would be ridiculous.

## Practice makes perfect

If you want to give yourself some practise in paraphrasing and asking questions, explain to a friend that you are keen to improve your listening skills. The friend's task is to tell you about something on his or her mind at the moment. All your friend has to do is talk – your task is to listen and from time to time restate in your own words what he or she has said, asking open questions to clarify anything you are not sure of. Your friend can correct your reflections and also tell you how it feels to be questioned. Continue until your friend confirms you have heard what he or she intended.

# *Body Talk*

Another aspect of effective listening is the way in which we can use our body to give the message that we want to understand and help. We can show our physical attentiveness through posture, gestures, eye contact, smiling, nodding and so on. If you are anxious that you might not be able to find the right words when you desperately want to be helpful, it is worth-while considering the other ways in which we can show our feelings.

## Stance

Leaning slightly towards the person rather than straining back gives the message, 'I know what you're talking about is important and I want to understand.' As in all things, don't go overboard! You don't want to appear so eager that the other person has to back off. Becoming conscious of your body language and controlling it is a subtle affair.

## Straight-on

Facing the other person squarely with your right shoulder to their left is another way of communicating your wish to be with them. The familiar phrase 'He/she gave me the cold shoulder' shows you how easy it is to experience someone as indifferent or rejecting just by their body position.

## Movement

What you do with yourself while you are listening is impor-tant. Good listeners move their bodies in response to the speaker rather than to their own feelings or unrelated external stimuli. The more deeply we are affected by what someone is

telling us, the more tempting it is for our body to respond –
nervous fidgeting, finger-drumming, shifting from one leg to
the other, jiggling a crossed leg and so on as we attempt to
contain our own strong feelings. These gestures can be very
distracting, and it is better to stay relaxed and fairly still. It
would be less understandable, even unforgivable, to do things
like continuing to watch a TV programme or some other
activity, wave to someone else in the room, nod to someone
passing, or look at your watch while someone is talking to
you.

## Eyes right!

Your eyes are also important. They are sometimes referred to
as 'the windows to the soul' and it is through our eyes that we
can most effectively communicate our feelings or intention.
Once again this is a matter of subtlety and balance; it is just as
off-putting to stare unblinkingly at someone as it is to avoid
eye contact altogether. Aim to focus your eyes softly on the
speaker, occasionally shifting your gaze away from his or her
face to another part of the body, perhaps making a hand
gesture, and then making eye contact again.

Sometimes it is difficult to establish eye contact.
Occasionally when we are with someone who is talking about
their deep feelings we look away from their face, perhaps
because we are afraid of being intrusive or of embarrassing the
other person. Although you might find it hard to look into
another person's eyes, think about the people with whom you
most like to carry on a conversation. Most of us enjoy being
with someone who has their attention on us rather than
continually looking at something or someone else! Lack of eye
contact can be experienced as a sign of indifference or
hostility.

## *How It Helps*

It's probably becoming clear by now that communication is not just about saying the right words to get your message across. It includes listening and attending with all your senses in order to understand as much about the other person as possible.

Let's take a moment to think about how this level of attention can help you. Careful listening and observation will help you understand not only the other person's situation but also how they are coping with it. For instance, someone might be talking about how well they feel they are managing their sadness, but you might notice their tensed shoulders, tightened throat muscles and clenched hands which perhaps tell a different story. Then there are the times when we use words or gestures to hide our feelings rather than reveal them. Have you ever answered the question, 'How are you?' with the words 'Fine, thanks' when things are anything but fine? We shrug our shoulders as if we are indifferent to something which is actually affecting us deeply. We smile when we are not feeling particularly happy. We might be very successful at creating a façade with our words, but it is not so easy to mask our body language. Our feelings usually manage to leak past our attempts to control them.

Noticing someone's body language is important to a good listener, because it's communicating what is most important to the person speaking. It's very difficult sometimes to put our feelings into words. Sometimes we aren't even consciously aware of what our deeper feelings are. Look out for these clues to the possible message behind the words you are hearing.

## Faces

Facial expression is a good guide to how someone is feeling. Eyes that are wet with tears, twinkling with enjoyment or glaring with anger are eloquent. Frowning, tightening the lips and so on all give clues to feelings which may underlie the words.

## Voices

There is usually more to any communication than the words which are spoken. In the first instance there are differences in tone and vocal quality. You can test this out by taking a simple sentence like 'What a night!' and experimenting with different ways of saying it to imply different meanings. The next time you are with someone, try listening to the pitch, rate, timbre and volume of their speech as well as to the words themselves. This will help you tune in to the mood of the person. If someone says, 'I've got a new job' with a bright, upbeat voice you can deduce that he or she is pleased and excited; however if the same phrase is said with a quaver in the voice, fear and apprehension are probably more to the fore.

## Gestures

A person's posture and body movements can tell you a lot about their feelings, self-image and level of energy. Our head, arms, hands, legs and feet can be very revealing. A tapping foot can signal impatience, while a nodding head can show agreement; however, you need to remember that these are only possible clues (after all, the tapping foot could just be the result of cramp!). Just as one word can have several meanings, so can a gesture. Gestures and actions don't happen in a vacuum – they are part of a pattern and it is noticing the pattern that helps you.

# *What Not To Do*

Before we leave this subject, let's explore some of the things we do which block our ability to listen effectively.

## Compare and contrast?

It can be tempting to compare ourselves with others to assess who is smarter, cleverer, happier and so on. If you do, you are constantly having to listen to yourself making the judgements: 'I've worked much harder than her'; 'He doesn't have as much experience as me'; 'She looks better than I do' and so on. While you are listening to yourself, maybe you are missing something the other person is telling you.

## Day-dreams

There are times when something that someone says triggers off a whole set of personal thoughts and feelings. A friend is worried about their child's behaviour and you start remembering your kids when they were teenagers, how they played you up, the time when you waited up all night for one of them to come home, how grateful you are that they somehow turned into reasonable grown-up human beings after all. . . . You are still there in body, but your attention is somewhere else altogether. You are brought back to the moment by your friend asking, 'So what do you think I should do?' So now you have to pretend you were listening all the time and bluff your way through an answer or own up to your day-dream.

## Telling your own story

Another temptation is to refer everything that someone tells you back to yourself. Someone tells you about their holiday and you immediately tell your holiday story; someone isn't feeling too well and you interrupt by describing the splitting headache you've had all day. Each time you turn the conversation around to focus on yourself you give the message, 'I'm more important than you.'

## Clairvoyance

Sometimes we think we can read the mind of the other person. 'I know she says she's tired but I'll bet she just doesn't want to finish the job.' Once we think we know what they are really thinking and feeling, we fit everything they say into our own picture, rather than listen to what it is that the other person is actually saying. We look for clues in body language, tone or intonation to prove ourselves right.

## Right on?

When we are sure we are right, we can become very argumentative. It's hard for the other person to feel they are being heard if you are too quick to criticise or disagree. If you are someone to whom being right is more important than anything else you will go to any lengths to avoid being wrong – twisting the facts, shouting, accusing, blaming and so on. You will find it difficult to take criticism or to own up to mistakes. This makes for exhausting communication.

One particularly unpleasant facet of this desire to be 'one-up' is the 'put-down' – using sarcasm to diminish the importance of the other person. We tend to resort to this when we feel most threatened by the other person. Someone says, 'I'd love to go to college' so you reply, 'What? With your scatter brains you'd never even find the entrance to the lecture hall.'

## Sifting and screening

Often, when we are tired or busy, we just listen for what we think is the main point, and when we think we've got it we let our minds wander. We can also filter out from our memory something we don't want to hear about ourselves – probably something threatening, critical or unpleasant.

## Nice as pie?

Of course there isn't anything wrong with being nice – but you can take it too far if you want people to like you. You agree with everything, but you're not really involved in the communication. It becomes more important to placate the other person than to engage with them.

## Practice makes perfect

When we are nervous or uncertain, we often practise in our head what we are going to say. This rehearsing takes a lot of attention as we decide on the story we want to tell or the comment to make. We're not really listening to the other person – we're listening for the gap into which we can place our perfectly crafted response.

## Label for life

The danger with labelling someone as lazy, stupid, incompetent, irrational and so on is that with these negative labels the person is written off – not worth listening to. Hold off judging someone until you have heard and evaluated what they have to say.

These are just some of the things which make it difficult to listen effectively. If they have suggested ways in which you sometimes make it hard for yourself, take a moment to identify your own particular blocks before turning to Chapter 3. Your increased awareness should help you avoid them in future.

# 3

# EXPRESSING YOURSELF

The previous chapter was about listening to understand as much as possible of what we hear. At some point, though, you will want to do more than listening and reflecting and that is what this chapter is about. If you want to give more than a superficial response and create a climate of support and trust, try to:

- listen carefully to the other person's total communication – words, body language, tone and so on. So much of our emotional experience is communicated in this way
- identify the feelings the person is experiencing and find a way to communicate your understanding of the feelings and their source
- get an image of the other person's world from their point of view rather than from your own; be more interested in understanding than judging or evaluating what is being said
- stay open and willing to share your own thoughts and feelings

# *Empathy, Sympathy And Apathy*

One word which could describe our aim is empathy. Empathy is generally considered to be one of the most important keys to good communication. When we talk about trying to understand someone we often use phrases like wanting to 'stand in the other's shoes', 'get inside their skin' or 'see the world through their eyes'. These are all good attempts to describe what empathy is. We can also define it by clarifying what it is *not*.

It is not sympathy, which is defined as feeling 'for' someone; empathy is more about feeling 'with' someone. It's not that there is anything terribly wrong with being sympathetic – we are bound to feel compassion and commiseration towards someone who is having a difficult time. However, unless some empathy is present, sympathy can easily become pity, conveying a sense of 'Oh! you poor thing!' which leaves the other person feeling weaker rather than stronger. Sympathy can lead to a kind of sentimental and self-indulgent wallowing in emotions which can leave people feeling worse rather than better.

## A healthy balance

Because empathy involves taking your lead from the other person, it can also be confused with apathy because it looks as if you aren't taking any initiative or direction. Apathy is defined in the dictionary as 'a lack of feeling or a lack of interest or concern', and that is clearly not what we are intending – although it's worth adding that in the kind of busy life most of us lead today it's not possible to relate deeply to all the people we come across. We have to learn to be able to keep our distance at times, otherwise we would become emotionally exhausted.

You could think of it in the same way that you might run your bank balance. Your funds probably won't run to letting you pay out for absolutely everything you want without replenishing the supply of cash; you would soon be broke. In the same way, if you expend all your emotions on others without giving yourself time to keep the balance healthy, your psychic balance will become depleted.

The notion of balance is useful because, while you couldn't (or wouldn't want to) become intimately involved with everyone you meet, it would be just as problematic for you to shun contact with everyone. To do this would lead you to a hermit-like life which is likely to feel empty and unsatisfying.

Empathy is like taking a journey with someone into their deeper self, allowing them to decide on the direction and pace. You stay alongside them, not taking the lead or falling too far behind. From time to time you might shine a light on a particularly dark place so that you can both see more clearly. The most important thing is that this is the other person's journey – not yours.

Your aim is to experience their feelings without losing your own identity. You can respond to their needs without judgement; feel their pain but not be disabled by it. The qualities which make up empathy can seem quite contradictory: we are talking about being emotionally close to someone while keeping our distance; identifying deeply with someone but not excessively. To over-identify with another person means losing our own sense of separateness, which in turn leaves us less able to be of help and support. After all, if you have broken your leg and are relying on crutches to get around, you need the crutches to be strong enough to take your weight. So empathy, then, is a kind of detached involvement with the emotional experience of another person.

As well as this ability to be close and separate at the same time, empathy also means understanding something of what has led up to the present situation. Being aware enough of the other person and their world to be able to see it with his or her eyes rather than with one's own; to know what life feels like for that person.

Finally, to be truly empathic we need to communicate in such a way that the other person feels accepted and understood. This is probably the most important aspect, because it would be counter-productive to put all this effort into understanding if the other person feels misunderstood and discounted at the end of it.

## *Can Anyone Do It?*

It's possible to learn to be more empathic, although there are probably some factors which need to be present in yourself in order for you to be genuine. For instance you need:

- a real desire to want to help the other person without controlling them
- a readiness to accept the other person and their experience as valid and valuable
- a belief in your own value and abilities
- a willingness to be 'with' the other person without needing to judge them as right or wrong, sensible or silly, good or bad
- a commitment to communicate as openly as possible

The thing that will help you most to be empathic is to stay aware that everyone is doing their best to survive emotionally, mentally and physically with whatever resources are available to them at the time. There are bound to be people whom you don't really like or of whom you don't approve, but remember that they too are engaged in the same battle. Some people have more physical, mental and emotional resources than others, and are able to meet life's threats and risks with greater strength, competence, courage, skill or acceptance. There probably have been times when you, just like me, have found yourself acting outrageously, inconsiderately, irrationally or even violently in your attempts to protect yourself.

It will help you to listen with empathy if you remind yourself that the person you are listening to is trying to manage their situation as best they can at the moment. If you are with someone with whom you find it difficult to empathise, try asking yourself:

- What need is this person trying to meet through this feeling/behaviour/decision?
- What could he or she be most afraid of?
- What could it be that he or she really wants?

It would be great if everyone had this kind of commitment to trying to understand and help others, but just having the right attitudes might not be enough. There are some people who seem to be natural communicators, appearing to key effortlessly into other people's moods and needs, saying and doing the right thing whatever the occasion. However, for those of us less talented there is hope. It is the expression of these attitudes which makes the difference, and this requires skills which have a strong impact and can be developed.

## *Silence Can Be Louder Than Words*

It's important to remember that there is no right way to respond to any particular situation. We already know that paraphrasing and asking questions can help someone express their thoughts and feelings. However, silence can be just as helpful.

There is a temptation, when we are trying to help someone, to talk too much: we feel that we have to come up with the right phrase of comfort or advice; we may want to distract the person from their grief or worry; we may want to distract ourselves from our distress. Yet attentive silence can be very therapeutic. Silence on the part of the listener can give the speaker time to think and the chance to explore thoughts and feelings more deeply. It gives the person time to experience and identify feelings which may be churning around inside. Silence also allows someone time to make choices about what to share and what to keep private. A therapeutic silence gives the message, 'I am content to be with you and to move at your pace. I don't want to push you beyond where you want to go now.' Great comfort can be found in the company of someone who makes no demands and accepts you as you are.

Many people grow up with the idea that silence isn't desirable. Maybe the idea starts at school when we are constantly pressed for answers or reactions. So for some people, even a few seconds' pause in a conversation can cause a feeling of panic and the impulse to rush in with questions, advice or comments. If you find yourself ill at ease when silences occur it would be worthwhile to try to increase your comfort level. This is not as difficult as you might think. Realising that there is a lot you can actually do during a silence means you can feel less anxious. During pauses in conversation you can

- *listen* to the body language of the other person, observing eye contact, facial expressions, posture, gestures. This language can often tell you more about how the person is feeling than words
- *think* about what the other person is communicating; consider what has been said; wonder about the feelings the other person is experiencing; reflect on the various responses which could be made
- *check* that your own body language shows attentiveness; keep your breathing calm; avoid distracting gestures; make eye contact

While you are busy doing these things, you won't have time to be anxious about the silence. You can say something like, 'I can't think of anything to say for the moment' if it helps you over your discomfort. It's everyone's right to talk as much or as little about their thoughts and feelings as they decide; it needn't bother you if the speaker doesn't want to continue. Some people think that if a problem is stated it should immediately be solved – but human behaviour isn't that neat and tidy, so don't feel you have to find something to say that will provide a solution for the other person.

As with everything else, it's balance which is important. Just as there is a time to stay silent, there is a time to speak. Excessive silence can be oppressive, forcing the other person to fill it. To sit in silence for hours on end without making any response is not good listening – it's just unresponsiveness. We need to learn to speak when appropriate, be silent as necessary, feeling equally comfortable with both responses. If you really don't know what to do, ask! 'Do you want to talk?', 'Shall we think about what to do next?', 'Is there anything you want me to say?'

## *Expand Your Verbal Horizons*

We have seen how you could respond with silence, with reflecting the other person's words by paraphrasing, and by finding out more through asking questions. Let's look at some ways of varying our responses. Many of us, unfortunately, have been brought up and educated in a culture in which it is not very usual or even acceptable for people to talk openly about their feelings. This makes it more difficult for us to feel comfortable in such a situation.

If this is true for you, you could give yourself some practice by increasing your vocabulary so that you have a greater resource from which to draw. For instance, supposing someone had told you how angry they are. You could, of course, reflect, 'I can see you're feeling angry . . .', but you would hit the target even more accurately if you could first determine the strength of the feeling and then use a word to describe it. Strong anger could be described as violent, enraged, furious, seething, rageful, wrathful, incensed; milder anger could be frustrated, aggravated, exasperated, indignant, worked up; weak anger might be irritated, annoyed, piqued, pained, peeved and so on.

If you want to increase your reservoir of words you could do this exercise by using a thesaurus and exploring some of the basic words we use all the time to express our feelings — words like love, joy, strength, sadness, fear, confusion and weakness. The more accurate you are in reflecting the other person's feelings, the more helpful the listening tends to be. The other person has the experience of being heard with care and consideration; of being heard with heart and head.

## A Good Answer?

If you are concentrating on reflective listening you need to be careful about answering questions. People often ask questions like, 'What shall I do?', 'What would you do if you were me?', 'What do you think is the best decision for me?' The problem with answering straightaway is that it's not always very helpful to know what someone else would do. That someone else is not living your life, doesn't have your experience, and won't have to live with the consequences of whatever you choose to do or not do. So, as a listener, it's probably more helpful to let the person continue to explore how they are feeling and what their options might be. Once you give your advice you may cut off the exploration, so it may be better to respond to a question by reflecting the feeling you think lies behind it. Imagine that Angela, who has a problem with a colleague at work, is talking to her friend Chris about it:

*Angela*: 'I tried to get through to him, but I just can't seem to make any progress. What would you do if you were in my shoes?'

*Chris*: 'I would tell him just what I thought of him and give him an ultimatum.'

*Angela*: 'Would you really? But I don't think I would have the courage.'

Now Angela has an added problem: she feels inadequate because she can't see herself taking this advice. What might work for Chris isn't likely to work for her. So here's another possibility:

*Chris*:    'It must be frustrating not being able to make him understand.'
*Angela*:   'You're absolutely right – it's not only frustrating, but I feel really worried that if I did confront him, things would be more difficult for me in the office.'

Although Angela doesn't have a solution to the problem, she is uncovering more of the feelings that are preventing her from taking action.

You will often find that, if you accurately reflect the meanings behind the question, the person nearly always forgets that he or she asked the question in the first place. Usually the discussion moves to a deeper level and the questioner moves towards finding a possible solution.

If the person persists and you do want to give your opinion or advice, it's a good idea to do so very tentatively. The problem for you is that, if your advice turns out to be right, the other person has learned that you are the one to come to whenever there is a problem. And if the advice turns out to be wrong, who do you think is most likely to be blamed? Probably the best advice for us is, 'When in doubt, hold the advice back!'

## *Short But Sweet?*

A common response to these kinds of suggestions is that it all seems to take so much time. It's true – this kind of response does take longer than a superficial expression of sympathy or a quick answer. So there are some points to consider here.

- *How valuable is the relationship?* With someone you really care about, one of the ways you can demonstrate the quality of your friendship is the time you are willing to spend with them.
- *Cost-effectiveness* Not to hear accurately or respond sensitively to people can certainly save time in the short term. However, in the longer term it can lead to misunderstanding or even conflict which could take a long time to resolve. If the other person is someone with whom you don't want or need to maintain a good relationship, it probably doesn't matter. But if that isn't the case, it may matter a great deal.
- *What if time is precious?* Lastly, reflective listening doesn't always have to take a long time. You can use these techniques relatively speedily to good effect. You can listen with understanding without entering an in-depth conversation or counselling session.

Caroline, for instance, watched her daughter struggle unsuccessfully with some homework, finishing by slamming her books shut. She sat beside her and reflected, 'It must be so frustrating when the work is very difficult and you can't work out how to do it.' They had a short conversation and the girl opened her books to have another try. It does make a difference if you feel someone understands how tough the going is; it's as if you are not alone.

Harry noticed that one of his staff was working particularly well, even though under a great deal of pressure, and commented, 'It's hard to keep going when the pressure's on, isn't it?' Once again, the other person is aware of being noticed and valued. One of the most common complaints of people who are working hard in stressful jobs is that their efforts seem to be taken for granted. It's easy to lose motivation when this happens.

Sometimes just a smile, a nod of the head, a wink or a hand on the shoulder is all that is needed to communicate empathy. These are only brief communications, but they can have results far greater than you might expect. You could try it out by resolving to behave in this way to at least one person each day.

## *Moving On*

We have already looked at how easy it is to offer advice which is inappropriate and which doesn't take account of the fact that it is the other person, not the advice-giver, who has to live with or through the implications of decisions. However, there are certain useful responses of this kind which you could make. For instance, you may have information which the other person does not, and which would help in solving or managing the problem. It could be foolhardy, even cruel, to withhold it in the misguided belief that it would somehow be too directive to offer it. It's worth remembering, though, that facts will only be useful if:

- the other person is emotionally ready to receive the information. Maybe you can remember times when you were told something but couldn't take it in because your feelings were too strong
- the information is relevant to the other person's situation
- you are sure the other person doesn't already know what you are about to say
- you are sure the information is correct

## *Actions Can Speak Louder Than Words*

Something else you can do is take action on behalf of someone. Although up to now the spirit of our exploration has been about helping someone to help themselves, there are bound to be times when this is impossible. If you are with someone who is too young, too ill or too emotionally upset to take responsibility for themselves, you may decide that action is necessary. After all, for a child of seven or eight trying to repair a broken toy, reflection on how difficult the task is will not be terribly helpful. Showing how to use the necessary tools safely might be more appreciated! A mother coping with a sick child would probably find an offer to do the shopping or go to the launderette as helpful and supportive as a conversation full of reflective empathy. Even for a person stricken with grief who would, no doubt, greatly benefit from the opportunity to talk with an empathic, reflective listener, an invitation to dinner might be just as therapeutic. There are times when actions do speak louder than (or at least as loud as) words!

## *What If There's A Problem?*

There may be other occasions when you could offer directly focused practical help. Very often, active listening responses are precisely what the other person wants and needs: the quality of attention and the space it provides are just enough to help the person to gain the strength to manage the situation. But there are times when it isn't enough. Sometimes struggling with a difficult problem is so draining that it just isn't possible to gather the energy or ability to resolve it. In these situations you could, if you wish, help the person without taking over the problem or the person. By active listening you can help the person through a process of problem-solving which will ensure that, as far as possible, all the options are taken into account and a well thought-out solution is reached.

Compare trying to solve a problem with going on a journey. To start with, you are in one place and want to be in another, if you have a problem there is a difference between what you want and what is actually happening now. So the first logical thing to do is to explore the situation so that all its implications are understood – just as before you undertake a journey you need to be clear about why you are doing it, where you want to end up, what methods of travel you want to use, what resources you need and so on. You can do this by asking questions like:

- What is actually happening now?
- How is it affecting you?
- How is it affecting other people?
- What would you prefer to be happening?
- What would you have to do for things to improve?
- Are these things possible for you to do?
- Are you willing to do them?
- How is that different from what you are actually doing now?
- What is the worst thing that could happen?
- Has this happened before?
- What did you do then?
- How could you/other people help you?

This type of open question gives an opportunity for exploring thoughts and feelings, fears and hopes without the pressure of having to reach a decision immediately. The questions take account of feelings without swamping the facts, and will help to separate fact from fantasy. As you examine the problem further it may become obvious that there are several factors, so the next thing would be to decide what to deal with first. You might be able to help by slightly changing the nature of the question. For instance:

- Does anything have to be done to a time limit?
- Is there a crisis?
- Is there any part of the situation you have strong feelings about?
- What would be easiest to start with?

And lastly, if the other questions are not particularly appropriate.

- What do you *want* to do?

## A New View

Having helped someone to explore what is happening, you might be able to encourage them to take a new view of the situation. It is very easy to get into repetitive thinking about a problem – you may, for instance, have had the experience of waking up in the middle of the night with thoughts going round and round in your head. At this point it is very difficult to create new ideas, but new ideas are probably necessary because the old ones aren't working. The most helpful thing here is a new perspective: another person often sees things differently and so can give new insights.

Janine, for instance, had been trying to manage her teenage

son for a long time. She was in despair because he left dirty
football kit all over the floor, never did his homework and
stayed in bed late – all the things which teenagers seem to do
to upset their parents. A friend said, 'It seems to me he's
behaving just like a lodger. Have you ever thought of telling
him you're going to start treating him like a lodger? You know
– charging rent, leaving him to do his own washing and
cooking?'

In fact, Janine hadn't thought of the situation like this. First
of all she laughed at the thought of it – which in itself was a
good thing because she had been so depressed. She began to
think more seriously about it, seeing how she had somehow
given all the power to her son, thereby draining her own sense
of power. This, of course, was not a magic solution – but as a
result of the conversation, Janine did feel better and started to
work out more effective ways of dealing with the situation.

Finding a new way to look at an old problem can lead to
new thinking and then to deciding what things to do. You
might continue your aid by helping the person to decide on
what action to take and supporting them while they carry it
out.

## *Too Difficult For You?*

Sometimes the person you are helping will need information
or a level of assistance which you are unable to give. Don't be
afraid to be honest – you aren't expected to be an expert on
everything. Your main role as a friend is to be a support, so
there will be times when you need to suggest that the person
goes elsewhere for the help they need. Many people find it very
difficult to go to a stranger or visit an unknown agency about

their problem, perhaps feeling that there is something wrong with them if they cannot solve all their problems. You can give reassurance by encouraging the person to get the help they need. Telling them that you cannot solve things on your own doesn't mean you are a failure – it means you're human!

In this chapter we have looked at ways in which you can build on your first responses to the person you want to help. We shall continue this exploration in Chapter 4 by discovering how important the words we use can be.

# 4

# THE POWER OF WORDS

No other person experiences the world in the same way as you do. We are born with a strong instinct to survive, but we have no information about the world in which we have arrived. It's like having to find your way around in a strange country you know nothing about. What you would need in that situation is a map which would tell you which direction to go. From our first moments we try to understand the nature of the world in which we find ourselves and begin to create a mental map.

Many things influence the making of this map. For instance, think how different the world of someone born into a wealthy, middle-class farming family would seem from that of someone whose childhood is spent in a one-parent family struggling to make ends meet in the city. Your position in the family, your parents' occupations, your physical health and your mental ability all influence how you see the world. Having a model of the world helps you to make sense of what happens, enabling you to make decisions and take choices.

To understand someone enough to be able to help them most effectively means understanding something of the nature of their own map, because even though you are both in the same territory your maps may be very different. We tend to believe that everyone else sees things in the same way that we do. For instance, you may know that what helps you most when managing an emotional crisis is to keep busy. It's easy for you to assume that this is the best advice for others in this situation and urge them into action. But they may see things differently, and their picture will make as much sense to them as yours does to you. If you push your viewpoint on to them they are likely to feel either that you just don't understand or that you are unsympathetic.

Have you ever been talking with someone as supportively and helpfully as you can, and suddenly found the other person responding as if you had unfairly criticised them? It's travelling with someone but having an entirely different map. You can't understand why the other person isn't on the same road as you. It can be distressing if your best intentions are misread, but one of the more uncomfortable 'rules' of communication is that the message received is the message sent. What this means is that, whatever idea you intended to communicate, it is what the listener hears and understands that matters. Sometimes the use of a particular word or phrase, an unconscious gesture or a particular tone of voice will communicate a meaning to the other person that you didn't intend. This chapter explores some of the ways that misunderstanding can arise as a result of how we speak and use language.

To understand something of other people's models of the world, listen carefully to how they speak and encourage them to reveal more of the way they picture things. You can often do this by making very simple interventions such as a question or comment.

## *Filling Gaps*

When we are explaining something we tend to leave out a lot of details – because we know everything about our own situation (or think we do!) we assume others will too. What we don't realise is that the gaps we leave are filled in by the listener, who is using his or her own model to make sense of what we are saying. For instance, someone might say, 'I'd like some help', meaning that they would like some support while they do whatever they are doing. A listener, however, might assume that they want someone to take over the task entirely. It's not difficult to see a misunderstanding arising between these two people. You can deal with this quite simply by asking for the missing information. For instance:

| If someone says: | You can ask: |
| --- | --- |
| I'm confused | About what? About whom? |
| I'd like some help | What kind of help would you like? What would you like me to do? |
| It's too difficult | What is it that's difficult? |
| I don't know what to do | To do about what? About whom? |
| Talking about this is hard for me | Talking about what? |
| I'm upset about something | What/whom are you upset about? |

## *Fuzzy Talk*

Confusion can also come about if pronouns and verbs are not specific. If someone says, 'It's so unfair', you are left to interpret the 'it' which could refer to any number of things.

| If someone says: | You can ask: |
| --- | --- |
| It's so unfair | What is unfair/in what way? |
| They are laughing at me | Who is laughing at you? |
| That's bound to lead to problems | What is happening that makes a problem likely? |
| I hate him | What is it that you hate about him? |
| They are so frustrating | Who is frustrating? What is it they do that makes you so frustrated? |

Another problem stemming from the way in which we use language is the way we talk about things which don't actually exist as if they do. People talk about 'my problem' or 'our relationship' as if these things exist in concrete form. They don't, of course, and different people may have very different interpretations of what a 'problem' or a 'relationship' is. The person who is talking knows exactly what they mean, but the listener has to guess. Guessing wrongly can lead to misunderstandings, so it is useful to try to get in tune with the person you are helping.

| If someone says: | You can ask: |
|---|---|
| Our relationship seems to be going wrong | What is it that is happening that you feel is wrong? |
| The children give me nothing but problems | What are they doing to cause problems? |
| I feel very rejected | How have you been rejected? |
| I've made a lot of decisions | What is it that you've decided? |
| You give me such disapproval | What am I doing that makes you feel I disapprove? |

## Saying What You Really Mean

Another angle to communication is the way in which we can cut off our options by talking in absolute terms or by apparently making assumptions about what is possible. Words like 'always', 'never', 'forever', 'absolutely', 'only', 'everybody', and 'nobody' have the effect of stopping us thinking about what the actual situation is. If someone says, 'I'm always failing' it sounds as if a decision has been made that leaves no other option. In fact it's very rarely true that someone is *always* or *never* something. So sometimes it's a good idea gently to challenge a statement, so as to help someone get more in touch with reality.

| If someone says: | You can ask: |
| --- | --- |
| No one ever values me | Who specifically isn't valuing you in the way that you wish? |
| People always laugh at me | Who actually is laughing at you? What do they say that causes you to think that? |
| She's always bad-tempered | On every occasion? You mean she's never been friendly? |

There are other words, too, which limit how we think. Consider the meanings of 'can't', 'must', 'have to', 'should', 'ought', 'necessary' and 'impossible'. When someone says, 'I just can't', they are implying that some outside force is making it impossible for them to act and that there is no other option. Saying 'I must' or 'I should' implies some kind of moral judgement, as if you would be a bad person if you considered anything else.

Challenging these statements can push people into imagining possible consequences of overcoming their fears or of taking responsibility.

| If someone says: | You can ask: |
| --- | --- |
| I'd like to go but I can't | Can you say what is actually stopping you? |
| | What would happen if you did go? |
| It's impossible to talk to him | What is actually preventing this? |
| | What would happen if you did approach him? |
| I have to keep everyone happy | Who do you have to please? |
| | How do you keep them happy? |
| | What would happen if you didn't? |
| I should agree with her | What would happen if you disagreed? |

Certain generalisations carry value judgements which disallow any other view. One person can talk about something being 'worthless', while another finds that particular thing useful. However, the first person appears unaware of any view other than their own. You can question statements of this kind if you want the person to understand that there may be other ways of seeing the situation.

| If someone says: | You can ask: |
|---|---|
| That's a ridiculous idea | To whom is it ridiculous? |
| | What is ridiculous about it? |
| Resigning was a mistake | A mistake for whom? |
| | In what way was it a mistake? |

# Twisting The Meaning

The map of meaning which we create from our earliest days and which becomes our habitual way of seeing things can cut us off from considering other alternatives. This limits our options, particularly when we are under stress. Here are some of the ways in which it can happen.

## Someone's to blame

If we believe that there is always someone or something outside ourselves to blame for what happens to us, we leave ourselves relatively little chance of changing things. For instance, someone might say, 'You make me angry' or 'I tense up whenever she comes near me', the implication being that these reactions are caused by the other person. This isn't really true, because our thoughts and feelings take place in our own mind and body. It isn't possible to put a thought or a feeling into someone else. You'll know that if you've ever tried to get someone to feel or think differently – they won't, unless they choose to do so.

It's nearer the truth to say, 'When you behave that way, I feel angry' or 'When she comes near, I feel my body tensing up.' This may not seem like a big difference, but in fact it is profound:

- If I believe you are responsible for how I am feeling, I cannot change anything until you decide to change.
- If I am willing to take the responsibility myself for my perception of you which causes me to react in the way I do, I have the choice of changing my perception or my reaction.

If you notice that the person you are talking with seems to be limiting their options in this way, you can remind them that they have more control than they think they do.

| If someone says: | You can ask: |
|---|---|
| You make me angry | What am I doing to make you angry?<br>What do you think I'm trying to do? |
| The course bores me | What is it about the course that's boring? |
| His insensitivity upsets me | How is he being insensitive?<br>What do you think he wants to happen? |

## Mind-reading act

Some people believe they know what we are thinking or feeling without directly communicating with us. The belief is based on the notion that everyone feels and reacts in the same way. People who believe this don't usually bother to listen or watch closely enough to notice that others experience the world differently from themselves. Asking someone, 'How do you know . . .?' gives them the opportunity to question their assumptions. For instance:

| If someone says: | You can ask: |
| --- | --- |
| My mother thinks I'm lazy | How do you know she thinks you're lazy? |
| The children think I'm too strict | How do you know they think you're too strict? |
| She only stays with him because she's afraid to leave | What gives you the impression that she's too afraid to leave? |
| Please don't be sad | What makes you feel I'm sad? |

## Less Is More!

Obviously, you can't go overboard with these ideas. If you were constantly asking people to clarify and explain themselves you would soon be seen as intrusive or annoying. However, when it's important that you understand someone as well as possible, and when what they are saying doesn't seem to make sense, is vague or misses out important information, a well-placed question can give you an insight into what is happening. Think of yourself as exploring a territory that is new to you, trying to understand the map which the other person is using. The more you can see of their map, the easier it will be for you to stay alongside them on this particular bit of the journey.

## *Listen To Yourself*

Apart from the words we use, communication is made by things like the pitch of our voice. When we are feeling intensely happy, frightened or angry the voice tends to rise; when we are depressed, exhausted or sad the voice drops. It is the muscles of our vocal cords which affect the pitch: as they tighten through tension the voice goes up; when they relax the voice drops. Listeners often make assumptions about you based on what they are hearing. A high, excited voice can be experienced as aggressive; a low, tired one as uninterested or uncaring. Vocal cords also affect the resonance, or richness, of the voice. Men, for instance, tend to have more resonant voices than women because they have heavier vocal cords and larger chests. The importance of this is that someone with a deeper voice is usually experienced as assertive, self-assured and confident; whereas someone with a thin, high-pitched voice can be seen as insecure, weak and uncertain.

Speed and volume also count. Talking speedily conveys excitement and expresses emotion. However, if you speak too quickly the listener can feel overwhelmed and nervous. On the other hand, very slow speakers can come over as uninterested. The positive side of a loud voice is that it can denote confidence and enthusiasm. On the negative side it can imply aggressiveness, a wish to dominate or self-importance. Softness can convey caring and understanding – but also lack of confidence or a sense of inferiority.

Emphasis also makes a difference. Try saying these sentences out loud:

- '*Is* this good news?'
- 'Is *this* good news!'
- 'Is this *good* news?'

Just by emphasising different words, the meaning changes from uncertainty to pleasure to doubt. Of course, every language has its particular rhythm which we learn as infants and integrate into our everyday speech patterns without even noticing. You will probably have noticed that foreigners often misplace the emphasis on words – unconsciously repeating their own first-language rhythm – and are perhaps misunderstood as a result.

## Check it out

Our own style of speech is so familiar to us that we don't usually think about it. But as a result of reading this book you might feel like checking on the way you come over to others. Ask someone you know well if they would be willing to record your voice as you carry on a normal conversation. This is better than reading or reciting something on your own, because it won't be as stilted. You'll probably be self-conscious for a short while, but that will soon wear off. Wait for at least a day before you listen to the tape, so that you can be as objective as possible. You are checking that

- your voice reflects what you want to say
- your tone, volume and so on match the words you are speaking
- you have no irritating habits of speech

If you do discover something that you want to change, keep practising with the tape recorder. Although it may take some time, it's not that difficult to make changes and you may find that your communication improves as a result.

## *Double Meanings*

When we speak we are often giving two messages. First, of course, is the information conveyed by the words we use, but there is also a message being conveyed in the way we speak those words. The way we inflect our speech, together with speed, tone and pitch, carries a meaning. For instance, a simple sentence like, 'You're home early' can imply surprise, criticism, pleasure, irritation or praise depending on the inflection. Try saying it to yourself and see how many meanings you can attach to this simple statement.

These unspoken meanings can be the source of a lot of conflict. For instance you could take almost any phrase – the more innocuous the better – and turn it into something which feels like an attack. Think about 'I was only trying to help'; 'You're obviously doing your best'; 'Do you want me to do it for you?'; 'What is it you want?' The problem is that these underlying messages are very difficult to defend oneself against. They are so subtle that you might not even be aware why you feel so uncomfortable.

Becoming more aware of the way in which you speak will help you to communicate more clearly and ensure you don't create unintended defensiveness or hostility.

## *Words To Avoid*

Some words have the effect of giving an extra meaning to a sentence and are best left out if you want to be clear. For instance:

- Surely
- Really
- Only
- Simply
- Naturally
- Now
- Hopefully
- Slightly
- Quite
- Again
- Certainly
- Suppose

Let's look at how some of these words can change or modify meaning:

| When someone says: | They are implying: |
|---|---|
| *Surely* you don't agree | If you do there's something wrong with you |
| Do you *really* mean what you've said? | I don't believe you |
| *Naturally*, I want to help | I don't really want to help |
| I'm *only* trying to help. | I don't want to be criticised |
| *Now* what do you want? | You're too demanding |

These particular words tend to create an undertone of disapproval or irritation. Test it for yourself by reading over the sentences in the left-hand column without the italicised words; when you do this, they turn into statements of fact rather than carrying an emotional charge.

## Why not why?

Another word which can carry an unintended message is 'why?' When someone asks you 'Why did you . . .?' it can feel as if you are being asked to explain and justify yourself, which in turn can easily lead to your feeling criticised and judged. Although this may not be your intention, a 'why' question often makes people defensive. Maybe it comes from being asked to explain ourselves so often when we were young that we developed the habit of believing that we need to defend ourselves against criticism. Whatever the reason, asking some-one 'why . . .?' often stops the flow of communication, so it's better to find some other way of asking. Words like 'how', 'what', 'where' and 'when' don't seem to have the same effect, so instead of asking, 'Why did you do that?' you could say, 'What led you to make that decision?'

## I love you but . . .

Another word better left out is 'but', because whatever comes before the 'but' is cancelled out by whatever comes after. 'You're looking good today, but what made you choose those shoes?'; 'That's a good report, but what a shame about your geography mark'; 'You presented yourself well at the interview, but there were one or two questions which you didn't answer.' You can experiment with statements which have a 'but' in them and notice the effect, which can be very dampening. It's a bit like being given a gift with one hand only to have it taken away with the other. To avoid this, you can train yourself to use the word 'and' every time you feel a 'but' trembling on your lips. Try with the sentences you used for your experiment, and notice the difference.

This chapter has been about the power of words – how an ordinary word or phrase can carry a world of meaning and not always the one you intended. In Chapter 5 we shall be looking at further avoidable pitfalls.

# 5

# SHARPENING UP YOUR LISTENING

Learning to listen is like learning any skill. The more you practise, the better you get. Think of another skill you have developed – perhaps you play a musical instrument. Remember what it was like when you were learning. You practised scales over and over again; when you tried to play the melodies you stumbled over the difficult phrases. Each mistake, though, helped you to get it right. You couldn't have improved if you weren't aware of those errors. Learning to listen isn't really any different. You can be sharpening your skills all the time. This concluding chapter in Part I covers points which will help improve your listening even more, and continues the theme of ensuring that we are as helpful as possible to our friends.

## *Don't Pretend*

You've probably at some time been talking with someone without really understanding what they are saying. Maybe you've been caught up with your own thoughts and lost the thread of what they were saying; perhaps your attention has been distracted by something you can see; the other person may not be very coherent; or your thoughts might have raced ahead of what he or she is saying. Whatever the reason, don't be tempted into pretending that you have been listening attentively and understand everything. Whenever I've done this, I've hoped that I could pick up enough clues to make up for what I've missed. Usually I've been wrong.

It's wiser to admit you've missed something and work to get back in tune. You can say something like, 'I've got a bit muddled – could you possibly go over that again?' or 'I got a bit lost when you were talking about the problem with the children – tell me what happened after that.' Although you might feel a bit self-conscious, the other person will get the message that you are listening carefully and want to understand as well as possible. Their response is likely to be more positive than you expect. Even if it isn't, you are in a better position than if you are groping around not quite knowing what to say for the best.

## I Know How You Feel – No, You Don't!

As you listen to someone's problems it's tempting to say something like, 'I know just how you feel.' You may have had a similar problem; you may be a similar kind of person, perhaps the same age, sex or background, or perhaps you do the same job. Nevertheless, however much you feel you are the same as the other person, you can't really know what it's like to be in their shoes. They are experiencing their situation from their own point of view; they have their own particular history, set of values, needs and wishes which influence their perception.

One problem with saying, 'I know how you feel' is that the other person might stop describing the details that would help you understand more accurately. Another is that he or she may doubt that you understand as much as you say you do, but won't feel able to argue with you. It's more helpful to show how much you understand by empathising in the way we explored in Chapter 3. You are trying to put over the message 'I am with you', which you will do more successfully by reflecting your understanding of the situation than by saying, 'I know how you feel.'

## *Ring The Changes*

It's a common experience to be lost for words, especially when someone is telling you something distressing, but there are a variety of responses you can make. The fear of saying the wrong thing can be paralysing – but there's no 'right' response to a particular statement. We have already seen how silence can be a very therapeutic response. You can paraphrase what the person has just said; you can reply with your own interpretations of the meanings; you can make a summary of what you have heard so far. Each of us has our own ways of offering comfort – a hug, a cup of tea, a bunch of flowers or an invitation to a meal are all symbols of how much we care; we don't have to use words.

Earlier we explored how to reflect what someone was saying; there are many different ways of doing this. For instance, imagine that a young father is talking about how he feels ignored by his wife whose attention seems to be entirely on the baby. You could reflect empathy in any of these statements:

- You're upset at feeling sidelined.
- Feeling ignored is like getting the message that you're not important.
- You wish she would involve you more.
- It's frustrating to want to help but not know how.
- Maybe it feels like the baby has taken over.

It doesn't really matter whether any of these statements is 'right'. What matters is the message that you are giving – that you are trying to understand. The other person's response will tell you whether you have hit the nail on the head. If you have, the other person will say something like, 'Yes, that's it' and you can continue. If not, the other person will be encouraged to explore further. They will say something like, 'No, it's not quite like that' or 'What I mean is . . .'. Their response will give you more information, so that your understanding can deepen.

## *Make Things Concrete*

When you are trying to cope with a difficult problem it's often very hard to talk about it. You might be embarrassed or afraid of being judged as weak or stupid; perhaps it's something you have never spoken about before. As a result people tend to speak in very vague or general terms, which if you are the one trying to help makes it difficult to know how to respond. You can make it easier for both of you by helping the other person to put his or her thoughts and feelings into words. If you continue to converse in very vague terms it will be much harder to come to any decisions.

Imagine, for instance, that your friend says something like, 'I just don't think I can go on. What are people going to think when they hear I've lost my job!' In order to make things more concrete you might reply, 'Are you worried that people will think you lost your job because you did something wrong?' or, 'It sounds like it's the last straw that people will know you're unemployed', or 'It's hard to think about going on when you're so upset at having lost your job and people might think you are at fault.' Each response is a little more specific than the original statement; the other person will soon let you know whether your intuition is accurate or not.

Another way is to ask one or two questions to find out more information. 'What did you think when that happened?', 'How did you feel when he did that?', or 'Have you got an example of what you mean?' are examples.

## *Do The Unthinkable!*

You might assume that interrupting is unthinkable, but in their attempts to explain things people can deviate from the point and ramble on about irrelevant matters. The conversation loses its focus and you will find it more tricky to know how best to help. If this happens, you could find it useful to interrupt – though, as a good listener, you would not do so in normal circumstances.

If you do feel an interruption would be constructive, make a short reflective statement or summarise briefly what you have heard so far. 'Hang on a minute, let me check I've understood the situation'; 'I just want to get it right, the story so far is . . .' are examples of ways in which you can interrupt to help the person focus on what is important. Your interruptions should be short, though, otherwise the other person might lose their train of thought altogether.

# Be Tentative

It's impossible to know everything that someone else is experiencing; at best we can only make good guesses based on the quality of our listening and observation. So when we are trying to understand what someone else is telling us it's a good idea to keep checking out our assumptions to make sure we haven't misunderstood.

The best listeners usually sound quite tentative when they make a reflection or interpretation. Their reflections are often phrased as questions, always leaving the speaker the opportunity of refuting the statement if they want; for example, if you were to say, 'Am I right in thinking that you are furious about this?' it's easy for the other person to say, 'No, that's not what I meant. It's more like . . .'.

Sometimes you won't know what to think; you might be confused by the intricacies of the 'story' or about what the most important issue is. At these times, rather than saying nothing and hoping that things will become clear later, you can say, 'I'm not sure that I know what you meant. Is it . . . or perhaps . . . ?'

# Building Up

Coping with difficult problems often leaves us feeling very inadequate and weak. It's as if the problem drains our power from us – and yet it is those very qualities of strength and courage which we will need most in facing the situation. You can be instrumental in supporting and building up someone who is feeling so bogged down in their problem that they have lost sight of their own resources.

Imagine, for instance, that you are talking with a mother who is experiencing problems with her teenage daughter. She says, 'I'm at my wit's end – nothing I do or say seems to make any difference. I feel so helpless.' You, though, know that this mother is a skilled teacher who has successfully managed to get through to the most intransigent adolescents for years. Of course, one's relationship with one's own children is different from (and mostly more difficult than) that with other people's children. However, the communication skills and strategies that work with Form 5D may come in very useful with your own Incredible Sulk! This particular mother is feeling discouraged because she has lost touch with her skills and authority. You can lighten the load, as you listen, by reminding her about her resources and abilities. She may not actually be as helpless as she is feeling at the moment.

## *There Is No Magic Wand!*

When someone tells me about a problem my greatest wish is to say or do something so wise that the situation will immediately be resolved. I really would like a magic wand to wave over the whole scene. But though this desire is very natural, it is entirely unrealistic. Some problems just don't have easy solutions.

However, although it can make us feel impatient with people who don't seem able to make progress, we need to accept that many conversations will be inconclusive. Don't assume that, because you have talked for hours and yet no solution has appeared on the horizon, the time has been wasted or your friend is uncooperative. The other person will often have gained a greater understanding of the problem through your talk together. He or she may be more clear about the alternatives, and at the very least will be feeling less alone and more supported through the contact with you. This may not seem enough to you, but for the other person it is likely to be an important ingredient in their search for a solution.

## *Resist The Quick Answer*

There are times when the person with whom you are talking asks you directly for advice and the temptation is to give it, particularly if you feel you have the answer. However, it's probably better to resist the temptation for the time being and try to find out what lies behind the question. When we give advice we are giving our opinion based on what we would do (or actually did) if (or when) we were in the same situation. Since we are not in the same situation, except perhaps superficially, it's debatable whether our advice is very useful.

There are several responses to the question, 'What would you do if you were in my shoes?' You could say, 'Well, when that happened to me, I . . .', but if you wanted to take the conversation to a slightly deeper level you could try to reflect what lies behind the question: 'There are quite a few ways you could go – it's hard to know what's the best thing to do', or 'It can be frightening to be confused about what to do', or 'You're puzzled about what to do', or 'How do you see the options at the moment?' Your aim is to help the person get more insight into the wisest course of action.

At times communication in this way will bring you closer to the person, and at other times he or she will just get irritated because they want a straight answer to a straight question. It's useful to remember that, when the crunch comes, it's the other person who will have to live with their decisions and actions. Beware of changing your role: you are there to support and help the other person to manage their situation, not to be an 'authority' doling out advice and then getting cross because that advice isn't taken. If you feel advice trembling on the tip of your tongue, hold back for a while. You can always give it later, but it may be more helpful if you are able to help the other person to explore a little deeper.

# What Not To Do

As we near the end of Part 1, let's consider some of the things which would be better avoided if possible.

## Criticism: 'You've brought this on yourself'

Some people feel that they need to be critical of others in the belief that it will improve them. Being critical comes from a negative assessment of the actions or character of the other person. When someone is trying their best to manage a difficult life situation, it generally doesn't help them to be told they are to blame or that they lack the strength or sense to cope.

If you do notice that the person is behaving in a way that will probably make things worse, and you want to point this out, do so in a constructive way. The Five Rs is a useful formula for you to follow.

### The Five Rs of Constructive Criticism

1. *Reflect*: Before you say anything, be sure that you are aiming to help, educate or protect the other person. These are all constructive aims, and if your intention is genuine the

other person will respond positively. If, on the other hand, you feel the other person should feel bad as a result of what they are doing, hold your tongue. People rarely respond cooperatively when they feel punished or guilty.

2. *Report*: Start off by giving a description of what you notice the other person doing; avoid making any personal criticism. So you would say something like, 'When you get an invitation you refuse it straightaway', or 'I notice that you haven't been eating regularly.' The 'When you . . .' form stops you saying things like 'You are antisocial/letting yourself go/uncaring/selfish/lazy . . .'. Such personal criticisms usually lead people to become defensive – probably rightly so, since these general statements are just your opinion based on your own assumptions.

3. *Relate*: Follow up by briefly explaining how you are affected by what is happening. It's important to separate how you are responding from what the other person is doing because it's all too easy to blame the other. 'You make me feel helpless' isn't really the truth. Whatever the other person is doing, your thoughts and feelings are produced in your own mind and body and are a result of your particular perception. You can demonstrate this to yourself quite easily by listening to a group of people talking about someone. You will find that each person has a slightly (or very) different response. Your sentence can continue '. . . and I feel/think/believe . . .'.

4. *Request*: You might have a suggestion for a better way for the person to act, or there may be something that you want them to do. It's helpful to people if they are given some options, and it's more constructive for you to be suggesting something to replace what you feel is unhelpful. So you

might continue: 'I'd like to suggest . . .' or 'How would you feel about . . .' or 'I would prefer it if . . .'.

5. *Result*: Saying what you think the positive result of the change could be is more likely to be motivating to the other person.

The first example in the 'Report' section of the table could be continued something like this: 'When you get an invitation you seem to refuse it straightaway. I feel sad about this, because I think that even though you are probably feeling down at the moment, spending time with your friends could help lighten the load. How would you feel about coming over for a meal this evening? I'd really like it if you would, because I would feel I was helping just a little to make things easier for you.'

## Analysis: 'You're only feeling this way because of your unconscious anger'

It's also not very helpful to have your situation analysed and interpreted. The popularity of counselling and psychoanalysis has led to increased interest in the underlying dynamics of our behaviour, which in turn has turned many people into amateur psychiatrists. My experience is that people don't like to be gratuitously analysed without their consent, however accurate the analyser might be! They tend to become defensive or self-conscious, neither of which is conducive to good communication.

## Patronising: 'You poor thing. I feel really sorry for you'

It's bad enough to be trying to deal with some blow which fate has dealt; it's even worse to feel that you are in some way inferior or weak because of it. Kindness expressed from patronage tends to make people feel worse; no one likes to be an object of pity, however well meant.

## Preaching: 'You should be thinking of how the others are feeling'

It's easy and tempting to take the moral high ground when you are listening to someone who is anxious and confused and, as a result, perhaps not thinking clearly or doing the wisest things. Usually when we use words like 'should', 'ought', 'right' or 'wrong' we are implying that we know best; mostly this just makes the other person feel more anxious and guilty.

## Instructing: 'You must do this now'

The only time when giving orders which brook no discussion is appropriate is in an emergency, when someone could be seriously hurt if certain actions aren't taken. But giving someone orders about how they should be behaving isn't usually very productive. If a person feels coerced they are likely to feel rebellious and resistant. On the other hand they might comply with what is demanded because they feel overpowered, but the resulting actions are likely be taken without enthusiasm or commitment. In any case, the person's self-esteem is undermined and they will feel less able to take control of their situation.

## Intimidating: 'If you don't do this, you'll have to suffer the consequences'

Accompanying your instruction with warnings about what will happen if they aren't carried out is unlikely to lead to a wise and long-lasting solution to the problem. Threats will have the same negative results as giving orders and instructions.

## *Moving On To Practical Matters*

There is a danger that, while we are trying to analyse how we listen and communicate, we may get so self-conscious about it that we paralyse ourselves. If you were to try to work out logically how to walk you would probably find yourself falling over your feet! The main point I have been making in Chapters 1–5 is that being with someone who is distressed can be difficult and stressful because you want to do the 'right' thing, but it isn't always easy to know what that is. Careful communication can help you to help the other person and to make it easier on yourself.

In Part 2, each chapter focuses on a particular situation with which you might be faced.

# PART 2

# 6

# 'HOW AM I GOING TO MANAGE WITHOUT THEM?'

*'I felt as if my life had ended. I couldn't think straight and I had no idea how I would get through each day. I miss her all the time'.*

Geoffrey on the death of his wife

*'I just went numb when I heard about the accident – it took me a long time to believe it had really happened. Now she is never far from my thoughts.'*

Alice on the death of her daughter

*'I feel terribly angry – I just want to rage at the doctors. I know they couldn't have done anything to save him – they did all they could. But it doesn't stop me feeling so rageful.'*

Catherine on the death of her father

There's no easy way to come to terms with the loss of someone dear to you. It's difficult, too, to comfort and support someone close to you who is grieving. That's the subject of this chapter.

Let's start by thinking about what happens to people when they lose someone significant to their life. Our lives are bound up with other people from the time we are infants, when our very survival depends on our attachments to others. The loss of a close relationship can feel like a threat to our own life. We know rationally that every human relationship has to end, that we will all die some time – but that knowledge doesn't stop us feeling pain and anguish when we lose someone important to us.

> '*We knew that her time was going to be short, so I suppose we were as prepared as you could be. But when it happened it was still a terrible shock. I suppose we weren't prepared for the actual moment and the emptiness that came with the realisation she was gone.*'
>
>                                              Geoffrey

Many books have been written about the bereavement process, listing the various stages that we tend to experience. Elizabeth Kubler-Ross, for instance, describes five stages that she believes bereaved people go through: denial, anger, bargaining, depression and, finally, acceptance. It can be helpful to know about this theory, because it provides an ordered way of thinking about what is usually a confusing and emotionally distressing time. However, a theory doesn't necessarily tell us what to do for the best to help out.

## *Be Practical*

In the period immediately after the death, what you can *do* is probably more important that what you might *say*. Various practical matters have to be attended to fairly quickly. However this, of course, is the time when the bereaved are often feeling most dazed. In her book *When the Crying's Done* Jeanette Kupfermann describes how she knew nothing about organising a funeral: the costs, local regulations and so on. She writes about her experience of being widowed and describes how important it was that other people took over those arrangements. In her state of bewilderment and shock she dreaded going through the funeral, and allowing herself to 'be organised' helped her to gain a little confidence. She felt numb – even her physical movements seemed to be happening elsewhere. Her friends were there to buoy her up, not to comment on her lack of composure or eyes swollen from crying.

> '*I don't really know to this day who did what. I just know that everything was arranged and there was always someone around to tell me what to do. I couldn't think of the most simple things. The whole day felt like it was happening to someone else. I kept waiting to wake up from the nightmare.*'
>
> Alice

Colin Murray Parkes, one of the first people to research and write about the experience of bereavement, points out that the bereaved person is likely to need help with the simplest decisions. I remember a friend of mine trying to make up her mind how she should dress for the funeral of her late husband. It was as if this became the focus of all her distress and confusion for a while. To me, it seemed like the least important thing to be worried about, for her the matter was of great significance.

# *Take Time*

What the person needs most is time: time in which to take in what has happened. This is when friends and close relatives can be of great help by taking over the practical arrangements. Helping out with the registration of death, organising the funeral and informing those people who need to know what has happened are all tasks from which the bereaved person can be freed. If possible, you could draw in other friends and neighbours to help so that the bereaved person is not cut off from his or her contacts and you don't feel that you are totally responsible.

People who are most valued during this period are those who are there quietly getting on with tasks which need to be done, making few demands. This kind of help gives the person space and time to grieve in their own particular way. You can make it clear that you feel quite OK with however the person wants or needs to express their feelings. There is no 'right' way to do this – some people keep their feelings very much to themselves, others find relief in openly crying or shouting with anger. In her book *Perspectives for Living*, Bel Mooney talks to several people about their experience of bereavement. Anna Haycraft (the author Alice Thomas Ellis), whose son died as the result of an accident, describes how on a couple of occasions she screamed out her pain and how that screaming seemed good, 'better than crying'. On the other hand, Chris Patten talks about how, on the death of his mother, he deliberately tried to make himself forget and get on with things.

As a helper you need to be prepared to accept, without reproach, whatever way the person manages their grief. There is a tendency for some people to pour out feelings of sorrow and anger, some of which may even be directed towards you. This is not because you have done anything wrong, but just because you are there! Reassure the person that it is healthier for them to show how they are feeling rather than bottling it up. Don't, though, assume that you have to force them to show their feelings or that you should distract them by cheering them up. Take your lead from the person, talking if they wish, engaging in tasks together or just being around. Think of yourself as making it possible for the bereaved person to feel free and safe to grieve in their own way.

You, too, will have your own feelings about the loss, and it can be reassuring for the person you are supporting if they realise you are not afraid or ashamed of allowing your feelings of sadness to show. Crying together with someone can help them feel understood and less isolated in their grief.

> '*When the nurse told me how he died, she burst into tears. Everyone had become so fond of him, you see. I just felt she was so close and really understood how it was for me. I suppose you could say it wasn't very professional of her, but I appreciated her feelings. It made me feel less alone.*'
>
> Catherine

## What Can You Say?

It isn't easy to know what to say to a newly bereaved person, but there are certain points on which many people, on looking back over their experience, seem to agree. One point made over and over again is that it is painful when the visitor is obviously trying not to upset the bereaved person. They avoid mentioning the dead person or anything about them; they say cheery things; they come up with clichés of consolation and so on.

Since there is no 'right' thing to say, on balance it seems better to be natural. Talking about your memories of the dead person might seem to be painful – but then grief *is* painful. Nothing will bring back the person who has died and so the greatest need has to remain unfulfilled – and that is painful. However, many people said that they were more hurt by visitors behaving as if the dead person had never existed than by recalling them, even if the recollection caused sadness.

Another area of agreement is that pity is the last thing the bereaved person wants. When you know someone feels sorry for you, it makes you an object of pity. You feel distanced from people, as if you were less adequate and as if the person who pities you is in a position of superiority over you. So although you will, of course, want to express your sympathy, don't dwell on it. Speak from your heart rather than offer trite clichés. Everyone to whom I spoke about bereavement said they appreciated visits and letters of condolence. Visits reassure the bereaved that they are not alone, and there is great comfort in the knowledge that people care enough about you and the person who died to take the trouble to make contact.

> '*I still keep all the letters and cards people wrote. Some came from the most unlikely people – but each one was like a confirmation that her life had been worthwhile, that she had affected people. People seemed to find very moving things to say.*'
>
> Alice

## The Mourning After

In the Jewish religion there is a traditional week of mourning which is called the *Shiva* (Hebrew for 'seven'), when the bereaved sit together all day. Visitors come and go and in the evening there is a short religious service. The talk covers the story of the death and memories of the person in life, as well as more mundane matters. Visitors bring food for the mourners, so that the bereaved can get through the first few days without having to worry about matters such as cooking and other domestic chores. People who want to mark their respect or bring comfort to the bereaved know that they can call in during this time without having to be concerned about intruding.

Jeannette Kupfermann writes that this time felt like a network of support, making her aware that she was part of a community who also felt the loss. My own father died some years ago on the eve of a Jewish festival, which meant that no *Shiva* was possible. My mother still regrets that she was deprived of that chance to mourn in the ritual way. Others have talked about the healing effect of the contact of friends and family. Having other people share the pain doesn't lessen it, but does make it easier to bear.

Even people who aren't particularly religious often find comfort in traditional ritual. The Irish wake, the Caribbean and Indian funeral and mourning rites all provide the bereaved with support and contact from family and friends. It can be more difficult where there is no particular cultural or traditional pattern to follow. People who could support the mourners are left wondering about the best thing to do – and end up doing nothing in case they get it wrong. In Britain you could easily get the idea that death is something not to be talked about – something to be dealt with as quickly and quietly as possible. The feelings of the bereaved, though, are not particularly amenable to being swept out of sight. Words are not always necessary. A gentle squeeze of the hand or an arm around the shoulder can sometimes convey more support and caring than any words.

Bereaved people are often amazed and frightened by the depth and force of their feelings, particularly perhaps those for whom emotions have not played a specially important part in their life. The sheer intensity of their sorrow, anger, guilt or fear can be so overwhelming that they fear they are going mad. You can reassure them that this is not so, and they aren't having a nervous breakdown because they are crying or experiencing unusual or unexpected feelings. Their response is perfectly normal and you don't need to be frightened of them or critical of them.

This is where someone who has experienced a bereavement themselves can be of such comfort – if only because they are not surprised by the responses of others. Although we can never really experience what someone else is thinking or feeling, we can recognise and make sense of their behaviour because it will be in some way familiar to us.

> *'I remember one day feeling so disoriented that I thought I was going mad. I couldn't make sense of anything. I went shopping but couldn't remember what I had gone for. Jenny came round and found me a bit hysterical. She just said something like, 'I remember I felt like I was trying to wade though a swamp and I didn't even know why I was in it or why I wanted to get out.' That made such sense to me, and I felt better knowing that what was happening to me had happened to others. It didn't make me feel happier, but at least I knew I wasn't crazy.'*
>
> Catherine

## *As Time Passes*

When the funeral and mourning rites have finished, family and friends tend to disperse and take up their own busy lives again.

This is when the bereaved person can feel most lonely. Their grief may be at its deepest as the realisation that their life has been changed for ever begins to set in.

> '*I thought that my life was like a jigsaw puzzle which up to now had been pretty complete. But everything had been thrown up in the air and all the pieces needed to be put together again. But there was a big hole in the picture and I didn't know how to fill that in.*'
>
> Geoffrey

People who are grieving often feel physically ill; an anxiety panic attack can feel like a heart attack. They may not be eating properly; depression not only takes away your appetite but makes it difficult to get the energy to cook something just for yourself. In any case, eating on your own can be a bleak experience if you have been used to company.

So another practical way in which you can give support to a bereaved person is to offer an invitation for a meal without putting a lot of pressure on the person to be very social. It doesn't have to be a dinner party type of invitation, rather an informal family meal. Make it possible for the person to feel they can be natural – that you won't be put off if they are feeling particularly down.

> '*My next door neighbours were great; they gave me an open invitation to more or less come and go as I wanted. I did go in for supper sometimes when I got home from work, because that was the time I found it hardest to be on my own. Sometimes, we didn't even speak very much and I left after eating – other times we sat and talked for hours. It was a great help over those first weeks.*'
>
> Geoffrey

## *On Your Own*

Isolation and loneliness are big problems, particularly for widows. Modern Western society is not particularly geared up for women on their own. Restaurants, for instance, are notoriously unwelcoming to lone women, seating them in the most uncongenial place and giving desultory service. Many women are afraid to be out on their own at night because of the fear of violence. Maintaining your contact with someone whose partner has died is very valuable. It is surprising how many people spoke about how people who had been friends with the 'couple' withdrew from contact from the single person.

> '*I remember feeling surprised at first and then really hurt when people whom we had been friends with for years slid out of contact. I didn't want to be the person taking the initiative all the time and so we lost contact. I still don't understand why dinner parties have to be for couples. One friend started inviting me to tea when her husband wasn't there, instead of dinner. Did she think I was a threat.*'
>
> Catherine

Psychologists hold that our attitude towards bereavement is heavily influenced by our own anxieties about loss and abandonment; and this may go some way to explaining why people have such different responses. Bereaved people have often talked to me about how the very people they thought they could rely on most stayed away. Though undoubtedly hurtful, this is easier to understand when you think about how the death, for instance, of a friend's partner can trigger off anxieties about one's own possible loss.

*'I couldn't understand why one of my best friends ignored me for a long time. I couldn't bear it, so I asked her why she hadn't returned my calls or kept in touch. She looked incredibly upset and told me that every time she thought of Rebecca's accident she saw her own daughter. We cried a bit together and then hugged. I obviously couldn't make it easier for her, but at least we were able to be honest with each other and I didn't lose another person who was important to me.'*

Alice

Even after the funeral, there may be practical matters to be faced by the bereaved person who just may not know how to cope. Jeannette Kupfermann describes how much she valued the help of a family friend who was a lawyer and who helped her sort out financial matters for which her husband had always taken responsibility. Over and over again it is this practical help which people talk about valuing most highly. My mother, for instance, has a neighbour who since my father's death has taken over the upkeep of her garden and about whom she cannot express her appreciation enough. Undoubtedly he has also gained pleasure himself, since he is a keen gardener and can now expand his activities. This maybe is a key to the most successful long-term help and support – that both parties should feel they are gaining from the relationship rather than one always being the recipient and the other the giver.

So we have established that the most valuable things you can offer someone who is bereaved are immediate practical help, acceptance without judgement, and willingness to use your own experience to help you understand how the other person feels. In the longer term you can stay in contact with the person – treating them as an equal person in their own right rather than someone to be sorry for or patronised.

# *Anything Else?*

Is there anything else you can do? Colin Murray Parkes makes the point that, while it is important for the bereaved person to grieve, it is also important for them to be able to *stop* grieving, and to create a satisfying life without the dead person. This is perhaps the most difficult area in which to think of helping someone, because there is no established programme for grieving. The point has already been made that each person has their own way of coping and there are very few guidelines. Perhaps in times past, when mourning periods and practices were more clearly laid down, people were better able to move through the process and then on with their lives. Even so, Queen Victoria never really finished mourning the death of her husband, Albert, despite the fact that in nineteenth-century society there was a very rigid protocol to follow. In the forty-odd years of life left to her after his death, she retreated from the public eye and always wore black.

We have already looked at how you might support someone while they are grieving. As a close friend or relative, you may also be in a position to help the person realise that mourning needs to end if their life is to go on in as satisfying a way as possible. You might, for instance, encourage the bereaved person to see a counsellor. At times like this, visits to a counsellor can be very therapeutic. Thoughts and feelings which could be difficult to share with friends or family can be discussed with a counsellor.

*'I was so full of rage and envy towards women whose husbands were still alive. I felt it was so unfair; sometimes I could hardly bring myself to talk to people who had been*

*friends for many years. I started seeing a counsellor and she help me a lot. I could talk about these feelings and she didn't seem surprised or critical. I found she gave me a point of focus; if I had a bad day I would tell myself that I would be able to sort it all out when I saw the counsellor. I don't really think she did "sort anything out" for me, but she really helped me to keep a sense of myself. The other thing was that I didn't want to keep on talking to friends about my problems – but for a long time that was all I really thought about. The counsellor was someone whom I didn't have to worry about boring. I didn't need to be fair and let her talk about her problems in the way I felt I should with other people.'*

Catherine

Helping someone create a satisfying life without their loved one is a matter of very fine balance. One of the things that all of the people I spoke to while writing this book agreed on was the pressure they felt from some people to finish their mourning as quickly as possible. People would ask questions like, 'Are you feeling better now?', 'When are you starting work?', 'Are you going to move?' They would offer suggestions like, 'Wouldn't it be a good idea if you got out more?', 'Maybe you should take a holiday – you'll feel much better.' They offered advice: 'Don't allow yourself to cry so much, it just depresses you', 'I think you should take up a hobby' and so on. Being told how you should feel was the thing that made most people angry.

*'I couldn't bear it when people said things like, "You shouldn't feel so angry and guilty", or "Don't feel so sad, after all she had a wonderful life" or – worst of all – "Time will*

*make it easier." All these things were probably true, but I
didn't want to hear them. I just felt people didn't have any
idea of how I really felt.'*

                                                              Geoffrey

To sum up, it seems that the best help you can give is to be
prepared to be with the person, taking your lead from them.
Support them as much as you can while they find their way
through this painful experience, giving practical help to take
everyday worries off their shoulders when it is possible.

# 7

# 'I NEVER THOUGHT IT COULD BE SO HARD TO BE A PARENT'

Many people would agree that being a parent is not entirely a bed of roses. Support from friends and relatives is very important to those facing the problems that being a parent can bring. For instance, here some members of a parents' support group are sharing their thoughts and feelings:

> '*I remember feeling sick when the doctor told us that Jane was affected by cerebral palsy. I think I had known something was wrong, but I persuaded myself that I was being too fussy. I just panicked and couldn't listen. It took me a long time to come to terms. I sometimes feel ashamed of how I felt towards her at that moment – I just wished she hadn't been born.*'
>
> Jenny, talking about her daughter who is now ten

> '*We'd been thinking that something was not quite right for some time. Ben seemed very responsive in some ways but not*

*in others – and we realised that he wasn't responding to sounds. I think we both felt worried but didn't talk about it to each other for a long time – almost as though, if we talked about it, there actually would be a problem. Anyway, eventually Ben was diagnosed as profoundly deaf. At first, I just felt helpless because I couldn't "make it better" for him. We were very lucky, though, because we were introduced to another couple who had a child who was deaf and they were so positive and encouraging.'*

Harry, talking about his son Ben

*'I wasn't aware of any big problems with the children – I enjoyed being a parent – that is, until Hannah got to be a teenager. It was downhill all the way from then on – I don't know how I avoided hitting her. I often felt violent towards her because she was so uncooperative all the time. Talk about "The Big Sulk" – that was her to the tee!'*

Sarah, remembering the time her
daughter hit adolescence

*'It came as a tremendous disappointment when I knew that my son was a bit slow at learning. I'd always been near the top of the class and I suppose I assumed that my children would be the same. I knew that I should be patient and encouraging, but I couldn't help trying to push him. I spent a long time blaming the teachers for not being able to get through to him, and then blaming him for not paying attention.'*

John, talking about his son Damien, who is being
assessed for Special Needs provision at school

## *A Disabled Child*

Life can be particularly difficult when children have problems stemming from physical disability, slowness in learning or emotional upsets. If a child is diagnosed as having some kind of serious physical disability, the parents have to adjust to the painful realisation that their child will have problems they never imagined. After all, even the parents of able-bodied children are often disappointed because their offspring has not turned out to be the model which they had in mind. If a child is even more different from these expectations, acceptance can be difficult and painful. Just as in bereavement, people go through a variety of responses.

Many people describe their first reaction, on being told that their baby is disabled, as disbelief, shock and numbness. It can take quite a time to understand all the facts of the matter. The condition affecting the child might be complex and the parents may have several meetings with medical professionals before they can fully appreciate the situation. There may be a long period of uncertainty because it may not be possible at the time to predict the long-term effects. The same difficulties arise in older children who have accidents or infections which can result in a permanent physical or mental disability.

> *'Ben had some hearing tests and the specialist came to give us the results. She looked serious and I knew that the news was probably not good. My heart started pounding and although I could see her lips moving, I didn't hear anything she said for what seemed like ages. I had to ask her to repeat what she said and even then I couldn't really take it in. When Shirley*

*and I talked about it afterwards, we both had difficulty in
remembering exactly what the doctor said.'*

Harry

This is a time when parents need all the support and
encouragement they can get from friends and family. The most
important support you can give is to keep up your usual
contact; the most hurtful thing for parents who are trying to
come to terms with their situation is when people seem to turn
away from them. So if you want to help, make time to be in
touch. Treading the line between being constructive and
appearing patronising is not easy but take as positive a view as
possible. Avoid clichés like 'Every cloud has a silver lining' and
so on which can be maddening to someone who is looking for
comfort.

## *Comfort And Contact*

Sometimes the thought of what is happening is so painful that
the parents take refuge in denying that there is anything wrong
at all. It can be very hard to support someone who responds in
this way. As a friend or family member, you can feel trapped
between wanting to give comfort and needing the person to
face reality. Many parents feel enormous guilt, believing that
their child is disabled because of something they must have
done or not done; their guilt can be tied up with shame and
fear that they may be judged as bad parents. You can refute
this, not so much by what you say, but by not withdrawing
contact.

*'The first few weeks when we brought Jane home were very
hard for me. I felt that every time I took her out in the pram*

*people would look at her and blame me. I lost all the confidence I had in myself; I kept going over and over things I had done when I was pregnant to see if I could pinpoint the mistakes I had made.'*

Jenny

Though usually totally unfounded, these self-doubts or self-recriminations need to be talked through, understood and then dismissed so that confidence can be rebuilt. You can help by listening, empathising and helping the person to come to terms with the situation. 'I can understand how angry you must feel' is more helpful than 'There's no need to be so angry.' 'You feel you're to blame and that's adding to your worry' is better than 'Of course you're not to blame.' Although you may realise that the other person's feelings are not rational and adding to their distress, you won't make them disappear by denying them. Helping the person to talk about these feelings helps them to put things into perspective more easily.

*'One of my friends asked me what I was feeling at a time when I was actually feeling very low. So I just let it all out and told her how much I blamed myself for what had happened. The thing I appreciated most was that she didn't immediately tell me that I was silly to be thinking like that or say something like "Of course you're not to blame." She just let me spill it all out and then said that if she was in the same situation she would probably be thinking the same way. Funnily enough, it was when she said that that I began to realise that finding out who or what was to blame wasn't going to help us at all. It was more important to think about how we were going to manage the future.'*

Jenny

Anger is also a very human response to a situation in which one's hopes and expectations have been dashed. The anger might be directed outwardly towards the world in general; to individuals – usually the professionals involved – in particular; or inwardly to the self, leading to the guilt and blaming that has just been considered. Once again you may need to listen and empathise until the anger is spent. You might find yourself in the uncomfortable position of being accused of 'not understanding' or 'being too rational and unfeeling'. All you can do is try not to take this too much to heart, just stay listening and offering reassurance time and again.

## *Healing Tears*

Another, perhaps more obvious, reaction is grief. Crying, compulsive descriptions of events leading up to the diagnosis or events which led to the problem, avoidance of other children, frenetic activity followed by bouts of passivity, and inability to concentrate are all ways in which grief can affect a parent. Once again, it is the comforting presence and listening ear of friends and relations which can help the parents come to terms with the problem.

'*I kept bursting into tears at odd times. I couldn't control it – I would see a normal child and the tears would come. I would be talking to someone and suddenly feel overwhelmed with sadness – more than sadness really; I can't describe it but it felt like I was falling further and further into a pit which I couldn't get out of. Some people were obviously embarrassed or upset by my crying; so that made me feel worse. I always felt a bit better after I cried, as if the tears*

*had washed away a little bit of pain. I suppose the people
who helped me most during that time were those who weren't
put off if I started crying; they just waited for me to stop and
then go on with whatever we were doing. I didn't want
people to make a big deal of it, but also I needed not to have
to control myself all the time.'*

Jenny

As a general rule, the British aren't comfortable with the discharge of strong emotion. This has its obvious advantages –
after all, it would be tiresome to have adults having tantrums
in supermarkets because they couldn't have the chocolates they
wanted. You wouldn't appreciate an employer who burst into
tears on not winning a contract rather than planning how to
ensure the company gets the next one. A surgeon whose hands
shook with anxiety would not inspire confidence!

However, the discomfort that many people experience at the
display of any emotion, whether from others or themselves, has
certain disadvantages to individuals and perhaps to society as a
whole. Tears are probably the expression of emotion that
people find it most difficult to respond to without embarrassment or anxiety. Yet it can be the most therapeutic experience
to be able to express one's grief through tears in the company
of someone who isn't disconcerted.

*'I did break down into tears once when I was with a friend.
He just put his arm round my shoulder and although he
didn't speak, I knew he was somehow with me. I guess I
could have felt ashamed since men are not supposed to cry –
especially when they are in company. But I just felt enormous
relief at not having to keep my feelings to myself all the time.'*

Harry

If you are with someone who cries, don't feel you have to stop them or 'make them feel better'. The best thing is to let them cry, just as you would let them talk. Mostly people report that they feel better as a result of the tears. You could say something like 'Have a good cry, I know you'll feel better' or 'Crying is like washing away the pain, isn't it?'

One of the reasons why it can be difficult to offer help and support is that parents sometimes limit their contacts, perhaps because of fear of people's reactions or because they feel too upset to want to socialise. You need to respect their wishes while making it clear that you are available if needed: 'I'm here if you want me' or 'I'll be free on Tuesday morning if you need anything' or 'I'm just off to the shops, can I get you anything?' The offer of practical help can be greatly appreciated, much in the way described in Chapter 6.

> *'My mother phoned one morning and said she had a free day and would love to come and look after Jane. I loved it that she asked me rather than arriving and just taking over. It was probably the first time that I had had time to myself and could think of something else. I just did ordinary things like having my hair cut. It meant a lot to me that she treated Jane like any other baby, not as sick or afflicted.'*
>
> Jenny

## Teenage Troubles

Living with teenagers ranks high with many parents among the problems which they face, and the support of others can feel like a lifesaver. Everyone knows that babies eventually grow up, but it can come as a terrible shock to some parents when their

loveable, charming cooperative child turns into a sullen, obsti-
nate, rebellious teenager. Of course, this doesn't happen to
everyone. Some children (usually other people's!) seem to sail
through the process, gradually turning into civilised, helpful,
social beings. Friends can do a lot to reassure a parent who is
having a difficult time that what is happening is a very natural
process.

It can be really galling for parents of troublesome teenagers
when they see their children behaving impeccably with other
people. You may be one of these 'other people' and in a
position to remind them that their children are capable of
behaving like sensible human beings. You might then go on to
discuss how the conflicts are about the children's need to
separate from the parents and that rebellion is part of that
process. You might be going through the same process with
your own children – who might seem perfect to your friend!
Sharing experiences is often very reassuring. This, of course, is
the strength of support groups where people with similar
problems meet together to talk and exchange advice and
information.

When a relationship between parents and children goes
sour, guilt rears its ugly head again. We think it must be our
fault because we are imperfect parents. It's important, though,
to keep a sense of proportion. Children have to make a
necessary transition from childhood to adulthood which
involves many physical and emotional changes. Sometimes
these changes come too fast and are too great to be managed
without conflict and confusion. For the parents, the problem
is how to manage the relinquishing of the control they have
necessarily had up to now. To become an adult you have to be
able to take responsibility for yourself, to make decisions and
choices about your life. It's hard for a parent to know when and

how to allow this to happen. Because parents have spent so long being responsible for the safety of their children, it becomes a habit to check on what they are doing. For instance, if things go quiet it's natural for the parent to think something like, 'What's so-and-so doing? I'd better just check, to make sure everything's OK.' With an eight year old, this usually doesn't create a problem – it can be a different kettle of fish, though, with a thirteen year old.

> '*I couldn't believe how obstinate Hannah became. She used to stamp into the house after school, throw her bag on the floor, raid the fridge and take herself up to her room. No word to me; not a "Hello" or even "I've had a terrible day." If I asked her anything, she either ignored me or shouted at me. It was like having a terrible lodger in the house, and one who didn't pay rent at that!*
>
> Sarah

It is natural for parents to be closely involved with their children. Obviously this is a good thing, because the relationship between parents and children is such a crucial one. But, of course, that very closeness can make it tough to deal with the business of controlling, setting limits and disciplining children as they grow up and become more independent. It is helpful to have someone to talk to who is not involved in the situation and who can help you to see things objectively. A friend can ask questions to help sort out what is happening and what options exist.

> '*What kept me sane was being able to talk to my friend Brenda. She had a really good way of just asking a question which brought me back to reality whenever I was at my wits'*

*end. She had children of her own so I never thought that she didn't understand me – most of the time our problems hit us at different times, so that one of us was always able to be calm and rational.'*

Sarah

## Asking The Right Question

The kind of question that can help is 'What was happening for *you* while whatever-it-was was going on?' It is a common belief that parents should be consistent; if you accepted a piece of behaviour yesterday, you must accept it today and tomorrow. This assumes that our state of mind is always the same – but of course it isn't. Sometimes we are tired, emotional, worried, excited, full of energy or exhausted. Our state will obviously affect our tolerance level and so loud music, for instance, will feel much more intrusive at some times than at others. It's easy to forget this and feel terribly guilty because we haven't been absolutely consistent.

'What actually happened' is useful, because when we are under stress the danger is that we respond to what we *think* is happening rather than what is actually happening. Describing the actual events helps to separate assumptions from the facts.

'What is it that *you* want?' can help the parent consider his or her own needs. Parents get used to spending a lot of time and effort trying to give their children what they think they want, and as a result can get out of touch with their own needs. It's not so much that you are suggesting selfishness, but just giving someone permission to take account of their own needs.

'*I was talking to someone about the things we were trying to do to help Damien. At the time we were spending most of*

*our free time trying to help him read and so on, and I was
getting very frustrated because we just couldn't seem to make
any progress. My friend said something like, "When was the
last time you and Jean went out together?" For a minute I
thought he hadn't understood what I was trying to say, but
it was the best thing he could have said at the time. I realised
that we were so tied up with Damien that we had lost our
sense of proportion. Damien was only part of our life – not
all of it.'*

John

## *Brainstorm*

'What choices do you have?' is a question which can lead to
useful exploration. When someone is coping with a problem
which has gone on for some time they tend to go round in
circles, thinking the same thoughts over and over again.
Thinking things through with someone else gives a wider
scope.

For instance, you can suggest a 'brainstorm' – which
basically means writing down anything that could possibly
be done in response to the problem, however outlandish. The
point is to generate as much creative thinking as possible,
so at this stage you don't have to worry about things like
practicality, possibility or even legality! Sometimes a far-out
idea can seem foolish but might hold just a tiny nugget of a
solution. Give some thought to each idea. Those that are
obviously out of the question can be crossed off the list. Some
will be possible and practical and deserve a tick. There might
be some left which are not possible as they stand but are worth
thinking about.

Claire, for instance, was creating much conflict with her

parents through her choice of music and the volume at which she played it. Her parents, with some friends, produced the following list of possible solutions:

- Play your own classical music at full volume outside Claire's door
- When Claire is out change all her cassettes and CDs for music you like
- Throw away the loudspeakers
- Phone the police or local authority
- Cut off the electricity
- Move out and leave Claire and her music to look after themselves
- Provide headphones
- Walk around the house with earplugs
- Take all music equipment, cassettes and CDs to a car boot sale
- Put a notice outside the house 'If you don't like the noise you can now hear please complain!' Encourage neighbours to complain and send them to Claire's room.

Obviously not all of these suggestions are desirable, practical or wise. But some of them are and are certainly worth pursuing. However, most importantly in the short term drawing up the list is a lot of fun and to help someone laugh reduces the tension they are feeling. In fact, most teenagers have a highly developed sense of fun and a great need for stimulation; much of their rebellious behaviour stems from boredom. Claire's parents liked the idea of playing their own music extremely loudly outside her door when she was trying to get a homework assignment finished. She came out of her room in a rage and when she saw her parents lying on the floor with enormous ear muffs on she just collapsed into laughter. She got the point and they came to an agreement about what was reasonable.

You might want to ask your friend, 'Whose problem really is this?' Particularly when trying to manage problems with teenagers, parents can lose their sense of balance with regard to who is responsible for the problem. There are some things which teenagers do which clearly have consequences for their parents' lives and future, and others which do not. If you are with someone who is assuming that the problem is entirely theirs, and their children's you could suggest trying to sort out exactly who is responsible for what. This kind of discussion might not solve the problems, but it can at least help to identify matters over which there is no point in expending a lot of energy.

Sarah, for instance, brought to the parents' support group the problem of the 'undesirable' friends which Hannah insisted on bringing home. The other members agreed that it was natural for a parent to want their child to mix with friends of whom they approve and who won't lead him or her into danger. But, they pointed out, it's also true that teenagers want freedom to choose their own friends, and this is often the way that young people demonstrate most clearly their move towards independence. The discussion focused on whether it was possible to separate those things that Sarah needed to take responsibility for from the things which she didn't. The list came out like this:

Hannah's 'problems':
• The friends might lead her into trouble
• She might find it hard to say 'No' to them even if she wanted to
• They are a diversion from school work

Sarah's 'problems':

- Worry about potential damage to possessions or property
- Dealing with rudeness or disrespectful behaviour
- The feeling that the house was being taken over by people she didn't like
- The fact that she felt quite frightened of the friends and wasn't as assertive as she wanted to be with them
- Her sadness that they seemed to be taking Hannah away from her

Of course, this discussion didn't solve any of Sarah's problems, but it did allow her to consider that some of the things she was worrying about were things that only Hannah could deal with. She could begin to shed the responsibility for those things, concentrating her energy on finding ways of managing the things which did directly affect her.

Being able to sustain and help someone through problems they may be experiencing with their children can be crucial because it is so easy to feel isolated. Sometimes the onlooker does see more of the game than the player and you can offer a wider, perhaps more balanced view. This in turn can really make the difference to a parent who is at their wits' end as to what to do to help their child or themselves.

# 8

# 'I'M OUT OF WORK'

'It was the biggest shock I have ever had; I was called in to see my boss. I thought something was up because she offered me a cup of coffee, which had never happened before. She said, "There's no easy way to say this. The organisation is restructuring and your department is to close." I thought, "Oh, well. I wonder what job they'll want me to do now." She said, "We'll have to let you go." I didn't realise immediately that it meant I was sacked. I didn't have a job.'

Leila, on hearing she was to be made redundant from the company for whom she had worked for ten years

'I knew there was a problem with the funding for the organisation, but it still came as a shock when I heard we were to go. I suppose one thing that made it slightly better (if that's the word) was that we were all in the same position. But I felt very panicky at the thought of not earning anything – I couldn't see how I'd manage. Then I felt even worse when I *realised I would have to tell Helen – I just couldn't bear to think of it.'*

Jack, who worked for a voluntary
organisation which lost its funds

*'I was sacked. I didn't realise when I took on the job exactly what it entailed and I found it very hard to keep up. I thought I would be doing routine office work but I had to make presentations and I really wasn't up to it. At the time though I could only feel terribly ashamed and I didn't know how I could tell people. Being sacked is like being told "You're no good, useless." I still go cold when I think of that time – the feelings of worthlessness are terrible.'*

Neil

Leila, Jack and Neil are among the many who have had to face the loss of their employment. Even jobs which in the past have been assumed to be absolutely secure are now much more uncertain. For most people, hearing that they are to lose their job is a great shock. Even if rumours have been going around for some time; departments reorganised, downsized or closed; other people leaving and not being replaced and so on, actually hearing the words, 'I'm sorry to have to tell you . . .' is dismaying. Jennifer, who worked for a company which closed several small local offices, remembers her very physical reaction to hearing the news: 'I started sweating; I could feel it trickling down my back. I couldn't breathe properly, my stomach tightened up and I thought I was going to faint.'

## Reacting To Imposed Unemployment

People react differently to the sudden loss of their job. One person might react with excessive activity to avoid thinking about the consequences; another with withdrawal and depression. There may be a feeling of closeness with others in the company who are similarly affected; there may be feelings of alienation. Trying to cope with your world being turned upside down is not easy. The first reaction may be not to believe it at all. No one wants to believe they are not wanted; that they are dispensable. Some people's minds begin to work overtime; others go blank, not wanting to think or talk about it. For many people the hardest part is to tell their family and friends – and in fact some people don't.

> '*I just couldn't say anything. I used to go out of the house at my usual time and take the train to town. I don't know what I thought I was doing – I just couldn't think about it. Every day was a nightmare – in fact, on looking back, I think I was a kind of sleepwalker. I was living – moving and breathing and so on – but I just wasn't present. Eventually, of course, Helen found out. I think she phoned me one day at the office – and of course whoever answered the phone told her what had happened. She was furious with me, but it was a tremendous relief not to keep up the pretence.*'
>
> Jack

The emotional cost can be high. In Western society, where deep feelings often have to be hidden, it's difficult to know how to discharge the anger which might be directed at the immediate boss, the director, the company or the world at large. It feels impossible to express the sadness, fear and anxiety; to describe the feelings of being out of control, helpless and vulnerable. Sometimes the feelings which are being kept down burst out to those who are nearest and dearest, who end up feeling hurt and confused. An even more harmful result is the anger turned inwards against the self, which so often turns to depression which in turn frequently leads to apathy and lack of confidence.

Our bodies, too, react to this emotional tension with ailments such as backache, headaches and stomach upsets. While the trigger for these symptoms might be stress and tension, the illnesses themselves are real, adding pain and discomfort to all the other worries.

## Adding Up The Losses

What actually is lost when employment is summarily curtailed?

### Predictability

Our sense of security is heavily dependent on knowing more or less reliably how our life is going to be for the foreseeable future. Without that level of certainty, life can feel threatening and dangerous.

### Sense of self

Our place in society and our sense of identity are often defined by the work we do. Having no work shakes our confidence in our skills and knowledge. How do we know we will ever get another job?

### Pride

Having a defined role in society gives us a sense of dignity and pride in what we achieve. Shame is often attached to the label of redundancy and, although people might be sympathetic, their sympathy does little to modify the feeling of not being wanted or needed. Unemployment still carries a slur, even though it may be entirely out of the control of the person concerned.

## Personal satisfaction

Knowing that we are fulfilling a necessary role by doing our job satisfies us that we are needed. If the job is no longer there it's much more difficult to feel we are of consequence to those people close to us and the world in general.

## Security

The loss of regular income is obviously a major factor. If we don't earn money, how will we keep a roof over our heads, provide food for our family and pay the bills, let alone provide for the more luxurious aspects of living such as holidays and running the car? Our whole lifestyle is under threat as well as the loss of independence which is important to many people's sense of well-being and confidence.

# How To Help

There are two areas in which we can be of most help. One is offering support through the emotional upset during the first few weeks, which means hearing and accepting the thoughts and feelings of the person involved and perhaps also those of their partner, who is equally affected by the situation. The other is to provide whatever practical support you can while the job search goes on. If you are helping someone who has been sacked you have a more intricate task. They have probably suffered an enormous blow to their self-esteem and don't even have the cushion of a redundancy payment to tide them over.

Supporting someone through the first few weeks of their redundancy can mean helping in a variety of ways.

## Accepting the inevitable

It's inevitable that unexpected redundancy will carry a sense of loss, with all the effects already discussed. You can give reassurance that the physical and emotional feelings being experienced are entirely natural. This can be enormous relief to someone who is not only trying to cope with the worries about losing and finding work but also wondering whether they are going mad because what they are feeling seems irrational.

## Loosen that upper lip!

Expressing feelings doesn't in itself solve any problems, but not expressing them can obstruct our ability to think clearly and take action. 'Keeping a stiff upper lip' can take a great deal of energy, and it can be highly therapeutic to be able to express just how one is feeling to someone who is not going to be shocked or judgemental. This is where a friend who is not actually involved or personally affected by the situation can be of great help. Most people want to shield their nearest and dearest from as much distress as possible, and don't want to overburden them with the intensity or confusion of their thoughts and feelings. To be able to talk freely to someone who cares about you but is not directly affected is a relief.

## Don't panic!

When faced with the prospect of unemployment and its implications, the temptation is to make hasty decisions born out of panic. Yet the apparently negative situation could possibly be turned into an opportunity for a considered review of the options for change, particularly for someone who was not especially happy in their job anyway. So if you get the feeling that the person is making decisions too quickly, you should encourage them to take a little more time to explore the possibilities.

## Take care

Losing a job can severely dent one's self-esteem, so it might feel more appropriate to punish rather than nurture oneself. Yet this is a time when we need all the energy and confidence we can muster to face the future. Every person has their own ways of getting to feel a bit better about themselves. Visiting a place of interest, listening to favourite music, going for a walk in the country, writing out goals for the future, making a list of one's achievements, meditation and going for a swim are examples. If you find your friend falling into a self-punishing state, encourage them to undertake some activity in which they can indulge themselves just a little.

# *Think Again*

Another way you can help someone through this kind of difficult time is to notice whether the way they are thinking is preventing them from dealing with the situation as wisely as possible. The way we think has a vital influence on how we respond to setbacks. Negative thinking makes it difficult for us to take positive action. There are certain patterns of unhelpful thinking which you might recognise.

- *Self-criticism:* 'It's my fault'; 'I ought to be able to provide for the family'; 'I'm not good enough'; 'I ought to have done better'; 'People are going to be very disappointed in me.'

- *Worry:* 'What if I can't get a job?'; 'I don't know how we are going to manage'; 'How will we pay the mortgage?'
- *Victim:* 'This always happens to me'; 'I can't do anything about it'; 'I feel so helpless.'
- *Be strong:* 'I mustn't show my feelings'; 'I can't be seen to be vulnerable'; 'I must keep on working.'
- *Blaming:* 'The government are responsible because their policies are increasing unemployment'; 'If management had been more competent the company would have survived.'

Patterns of thinking of this kind often come from the negative beliefs we can develop as we are growing up. These beliefs increase the worry, anger, fear, depression or guilt that people experience. They include:

- I must be perfect in all I do
- I can never control what happens to me
- It's better to hide from conflict because it will always be painful
- It's impossible for people, including me, to change
- I will never be good enough
- People are fragile and should be protected from the truth if it's unpleasant
- Crises are always destructive; no good ever comes from them
- I must keep everyone pleased all the time

Thinking in this kind of way makes it very difficult to contemplate positive action. If you hear your friend talking like this, you could challenge them and encourage more constructive 'self-talk'. Be on the look-out for generalisations like:

- *No one* will want to employ me
- I'll *never* get another job
- *Everyone* looks down on me

Words like 'all', 'every', 'never', 'nobody', 'everybody' and 'always' are often clues that the person is perceiving reality through distorted thinking habits. Once you think that something will *never* happen, what point is there in making constructive plans? If you are convinced that you will *always* have a problem, how can you begin to create a solution?

This kind of thinking can also take the form of stereotyping – applying a description to a whole class of people, things or experiences:

- Employers are all the same; none of them are interested in their employees
- I'm a failure at everything
- In the end, everyone is out for themselves

You can refuse to accept these statements. Asking questions like 'What evidence do you have for that conclusion?' or 'How can you be sure that it will *never/always* be so?' can encourage the person to create more possibilities by thinking less in absolute terms.

There are some other destructive thinking habits which you might notice:

## Selective deafness

This is a way of filtering reality so that we only see our world through the darkest lens. I remember talking with an actor whose play had just opened. He had just read the reviews, of which ten were extremely complimentary. However, one critic did not like either the play or my client's performance and it was this one which took up all his attention. He felt let down and incompetent. The ten glowing accounts were no consolation – in fact my client didn't even remember them. It was as if he had never read them.

You should suspect this is happening if you hear your friend use words like 'unfair', 'stupid', 'hurt', 'incompetent', 'untalented' or 'silly'. Focusing only on the negative side of life makes us lose track of the whole picture. You can help to fight this by looking for a more balanced view. 'Hang on, let's look at the whole picture'; or 'Is there any advantage to what's happening?'; or 'There you go again, only seeing the bad side.'

## Either/or

This is polarised thinking, in which everything and everybody is judged through absolutes. Other people are either saints or sinners, heroes or villains, beautiful or ugly; when judging ourselves we are either clever or stupid, good or bad, successes or failures. The world is seen as black and white, with no shades of grey in-between. Self-esteem is bound to take a dive if we see only the negative side when things are going wrong.

If you hear statements like 'This is my big chance. If I don't get this job, I'll never get one' or 'Either he'll like me or hate me', it's worth challenging them and encouraging the person to see that the truth of the situation lies somewhere in-between.

Once again you can rebut this way of seeing the world. Encouraging the person to be specific is one way of doing this. For example, 'Just a minute, let's be more precise about exactly what is available' or 'How do you know that these are the only two possibilities?'

## It's all my fault

Self-blaming is another distorted thinking style in which the person blames themselves for everything that happens, whether they are actually at fault or not. They see only their shortcomings; they take the blame for things that are only marginally under their control, or even things that are completely outside their control.

The problem here is that, if you feel you are to blame for everything, you lose sight of your good qualities and accomplishments. Many people become unemployed because of things outside their control – for instance their firm may close because of a downturn in the economy; their job may become redundant because of the introduction of new technology. If, however, they can only see the situation in the light of their own failure it will become increasingly difficult for them to think positively and take action regarding the future.

Pick out judgemental statements and suggest more balanced ones; 'Everyone makes mistakes – it's just human'; 'You know you were doing your best with the resources you had at the time'; 'Don't let's brood on the past, we can't change it'; 'How can you be responsible for what others choose to do?'

## It's nothing to do with me

This is the other side of the coin, with the person believing they have no influence on their lives at all. It seems as if everyone is ganging up to make life impossible, and it becomes difficult to make plans for taking charge. This feeling of having no control also leads to low self-esteem and a sense of hopelessness.

Remind the person of the resources they have. 'Hey, remember when you were bringing up three kids under five? You certainly took charge then!'; 'What's the first thing we could do?'; 'Don't try to do everything at once. We'll make a list and then decide where to start.'

## Practically speaking

There are also simple ways of giving practical help, if you wish to and are in a position to offer. For instance, you might be able to offer space to someone whose accommodation does not allow them to set up a place where they will be uninterrupted. You might have a spare typewriter or word processor which could be invaluable to someone applying for jobs.

Helping to draw up a list of contacts who could be telephoned or written to and who might know of another opening can be very useful. You could help in drafting letters or 'role playing' telephone calls.

Give assistance, too, in drawing up a list of organisations or companies to which speculative letters could be sent. It might even be possible to find out the names of individuals to whom the letters could be addressed.

The person will probably need to draft a new CV; to help, you will find various useful books in your local public library. You can also assist by scanning local and national newspapers or specialist publications for suitable jobs which can be applied for.

You might also obtain information from local colleges, many of which run part-time courses in a wide range of career development issues. Many local authorities, too, offer training opportunities.

Mostly, of course, you can help by just being there – to talk, encourage, support, challenge.

*'I was shocked at how some of my friends just faded out of the picture. It was as if I had become a non-person and they*

*didn't want to know me. I still can't work out why they acted this way, but it had a profound effect on me. I suppose it confirmed my idea that I was somehow to blame for what had happened and had something to feel ashamed of. Of course, some people didn't treat me any differently from before – and they became so important. The people I appreciated most didn't treat me with kid gloves; they gave me practical help if they could, but most of all they continued including me in their lives.'*

Leila

# 9

# 'I DON'T KNOW WHAT CAME OVER ME'

*'What I dream about is getting out of office work and trying my luck as a singer, but I'd never have the courage.'*

*'I was so angry that I jumped up and down with rage.'*

*'I want to change my job but I can't cope with interviews – I just turn to jelly. I don't even hear the questions, let alone answer them!'*

*'I can't stand the idea of getting old – I'm really frightened of losing my soundness of body and mind and getting feeble and ill.'*

*'I'd like to tell my husband exactly what I think of the way he treats me, but every time I think about doing it I get so mad I can't think straight.'*

*'I feel so sad. I can't imagine life without him.'*

These people are all talking about how controlling feelings can be. If you have ever been so overtaken by your own that you can hardly speak, let alone think clearly, you won't have much trouble in understanding these people. This chapter is about the way in which our feelings can prevent us responding to life in the way we want, and how we could help other people overcome emotional barriers which may be hindering them.

## *What Are Feelings For?*

Feelings are our reaction to the world around us. They reflect our own particular history and development – those things which have influenced us in our past, our present problems, our hopes and fears regarding the future. The way we perceive things comes out of our own needs, hopes, fears and expectations. This is why no two people respond to a situation in exactly the same way, but there are enough common factors for a language to have developed for describing our experience of the world.

Just as there are three primary colours, out of which all the other colours are formed, there are four primary feelings:

- anger
- fear
- sadness
- joy

These are sometimes referred to as 'mad', 'bad', 'sad' and 'glad'. All the emotions we experience are a degree or a mixture of these.

## Past, present and future

Although not always pleasant to experience, anger, fear and sadness do help us solve some of our problems. Fear, for instance, is what we feel when our *future* security is threatened. This future can be very close; I may be walking down a dark, deserted street and hear footsteps behind me. The fear I feel is linked to the possibility of a future attack, and so I am galvanised into walking more speedily.

Anger is our response to a sense of loss of control of the *present*. Perhaps I have spotted a good parking space and while I am lining myself up another car nips in. I am angry because I have momentarily lost control of the ordered world where I can put my car in the place I decide.

Sadness helps us over painful events which have happened in the *past*. As we allow ourselves to grieve, to cry and talk about the loss, we begin to free ourselves from the past pain.

The fourth feeling, happiness or its more extreme form, joy, is what we feel when we have no need to make a change. When we are not feeling threatened, when our world is in order and we feel in control of it and the past is not weighing us down – then we can say we are happy. What makes each of us feel mad, bad, sad or glad is a matter of our individual needs and personality.

## *Thoughts And Feelings In The Balance*

The language we use to describe our feelings helps us to manage them; the words help us to distance ourselves from the experience. When we feel pain, we just know we hurt. As we think about it we can explain the hurt to ourselves by justifying, rationalising and trying to put it in perspective, but we can't diminish the actual feeling we experienced.

Intelligence is no particular advantage in understanding feelings. For some people, high intelligence is actually a handicap because they can use logic to obscure the truth of the heart of the experience. You may have met very intelligent people who don't seem to understand or place much value on their own or other people's feelings. As a result they make unsatisfying companions. Such people seem to be more comfortable functioning within the narrow confines of their intellectual system, viewing and commenting on the world knowingly, often with elegance, wit and grace, but somehow remaining outside mainstream human feeling.

It seems to me that the world is too complicated to rely solely on logic to evaluate our experience. On the other hand, to base our evaluation of the world entirely on our feelings is just as likely to distort our perceptions. For each of us the world is like a jigsaw puzzle which we must try to assemble to make a coherent picture. We can deal with it more effectively by using all our abilities. Being in touch with our feelings is as important as being able to make intellectual sense of what we are experiencing.

## The Physiology Of Pain

In the physical sense, it is our nervous system which keeps control of all the body's activities. Our five senses, touch, taste, sight, smell and hearing, are constantly sending information to the brain via an intricate system of nerves. We become aware of physical pain when a sensory nerve is overloaded beyond its normal capacity. For instance, if pressure becomes too severe, the temperature too extreme or sound too loud we no longer experience just pressure, temperature or sound – we feel pain. An electrical current is initiated in the nerve ending and sent along to the brain. The painful impulse causes us to move the threatened part of the body away from danger, if we can. We wriggle our toes in the too tight shoes, we pull our arm away from the boiling kettle, we cover our ears.

## Feelings As A Defence

We try to protect ourselves from painful feelings in the same way. Our 'feeling' system can become overloaded just as our physical system does. We can over-react to painful feelings by setting up strong defences which have the effect of separating us from our pain. There are bound to be times when we need a defence to protect us against further injury and give us distance and time. The problem is that the defences can be so efficient that we lose sight of the original problem. In earlier chapters, if you remember, denial was identified as one of the natural responses to loss and shock.

## Supporting Someone Close

We need to find a balance between pain and defence. It's generally accepted that the more we are willing to face and feel painful emotions, the sooner they will change or dissipate. This is a process through which you can support someone close to you. It may take courage to be with someone who is in intense emotional pain, but it's worth it in the end. To be free of the burden of defences that have their roots in fear and pain is a freedom worth working for. It means having more energy for meeting life with creativity and strength. This, of course, is the rationale behind the development of the counselling and psychotherapy network which is gaining much ground at the present time.

What we feel now is sometimes heavily influenced by unsettled events of the past. Counsellors can help people settle the pain of the past and free them to look back so that they can put the details of their lives into perspective. The way to continuing growth and development is then open.

When we were children, trying to get our 'jigsaw' of life together, we had to confront certain issues. For instance, when we are born and for quite a time afterwards we are totally dependent – we have to learn how to attain independence; early in our lives we are controlled by others – learning how to achieve freedom is the task; we have to discover our identity; we have to come to terms with acceptance and rejection, and so on. For many of us elements of these issues remain unresolved and constantly reappear as conflicts in our lives which we struggle to understand and manage.

This goes some way to explaining why we sometimes react with intense emotion to a situation which, when reviewed in the cold light of day, really doesn't seem to merit such a response. It's as if we are really responding to the past problem rather than the present situation. The complication here is that we can't solve the problem from the past because the past has gone, and we don't solve the problem of the present because our reaction isn't actually related to it.

Counselling has already been mentioned. If the problem is severe, finding a counsellor to help sort through the confusion is one possible action to take – and you might want to suggest this idea to someone whom you are trying to help. On the other hand, you don't need to be a psychotherapist to be able to respond helpfully to a friend who is in the grip of difficult or painful feelings.

Let's consider some of the feelings that can be hard to manage, and possible ways to help someone cope.

## Anxiety

We feel anxious when we are afraid of being hurt or losing something, and our anxiety can range from mild apprehension to utter panic. Whether the fear is real or imagined, it feels the same. Fear alerts us to the need to defend ourselves. When we sense a threat, our body releases powerful stimulating hormones into the bloodstream. As a result our heart beats more rapidly and the blood flows to where it's needed most – to the muscles, and away from the abdomen and skin. The 'cold feet', 'butterflies in the stomach', sweating and skin pallor we experience when we are anxious are all caused by the action of these hormones.

Our greatest anxiety is, of course, losing our life, and the physical response I have just described evolved far back in the history of the human race, when survival depended on the ability to fight a threat or flee from it, as already discussed in Chapter 1. For Stone Age people this made good sense, for life was a simple matter of surviving long enough to procreate and nurture one's young. However, in our world potential aggressors are seldom so clearly defined as those faced by our distant ancestors.

So how could you help someone who tells you they are too anxious or afraid to manage whatever is happening in their life? The first thing is to face something which might be very disappointing, both to you and to the person you are trying to help. You can't actually make someone else's fear go away. But what you can do is help them face and overcome their fear.

To begin with, you can establish some certainties about fear. This in itself must be a good thing, since uncertainty is one of the things which stimulates fear. For instance, it is certain that:

- *Fear is an inevitable part of change.* There's no point in waiting for the fear to go away before you take a risk. In order for us to feel absolutely safe, we need to predict the future. When we know exactly what is going to happen we can relax because we feel in control – but any hint of impending change will propel us into the fight/flight response because change, even for the better, carries some level of unpredictability with it. So rather than trying to talk your friend out of their fear, you can reassure them that what they are feeling is entirely natural. It can come as a tremendous relief to know that you aren't a weak little worm for feeling as you do, and that it need not stop you moving forward.

- *The only way really to get rid of a fear of doing something is to go and do it.* If you are with someone who is talking about their fear of something which they would like to do, encourage them to do it (providing of course it's safe and legal!).

  If you think the person might be imagining all sorts of disasters which could come about if they took action, encourage them to start in spite of the risk. Many of us have the kind of imagination which works like a soap opera – each event we create in our mind ends in disaster! A good question is 'What is the worst that could happen?' Articulating the worst fear allows it to be put in perspective. Sometimes the worst thing that could happen is that nothing will change as a result of the action. If so, you can point out that this means the person can lose nothing by taking action and at the very least they will know they had a go.

- *Everyone experiences fear when they are in unfamiliar territory.* This is something else you can tell the person you are helping. Most people don't want to let others know that they are or have been afraid, so they appear to be moving ahead in their lives with supreme confidence. It's true that some people are better than others at not letting their fear stop them, but it isn't true that there are people who never experience fear. It's important to know that you are not alone.

- *Letting yourself be controlled by fear is more frightening than taking control.* For some people life is full of the fear and anxiety induced by the question 'What if . . .'. It's so easy to build up a fantasy future full of hopelessness and helplessness: 'What if I get ill/become disabled/lose my partner/lose my job.' Letting these fears rule our lives means using a great deal of our energy to protect us from our fantasy of the future, leaving less for managing the present. The irony is that people who refuse to take risks live with a feeling of dread that is likely to be far worse than anything they would feel if they actually took some of these risks.

*'I remember standing in front of the class of kids who weren't that much younger than me at the time. I had been up all night going over and over the lesson I had prepared. I had enough material for a three-week course, but I was so frightened of looking as if I didn't know what I was doing that I had programmed every second with activity.*

*I got to the classroom early and remember waiting for*

*them to arrive. I played with the idea of leaving before they came. I thought I could give it all up now and go in for something much less stressful. I felt sick and my hands were sweating. As they came in I could feel my heart beating and my knees shaking. I could hardly write on the board because my hands were shaking so much.*

*Anyway, I got through it somehow. I didn't faint; my voice didn't give out; the kids didn't riot or fall about laughing – all things I had imagined might happen!*

*That was definitely the worst time – each time it got easier and I felt more confident. The second class felt easier than the first, and the third felt better than the second, and so on. Eventually, I began to enjoy working with the kids and actually looked forward to seeing them.*

*I can't deny that there are still times when I'm scared – some classes are truly frightening! But I know I can cope and that's the most important thing. I feel in control of myself and I know I can do it.'*

Malcolm, talking about his first experience<br>as a young teacher

Barbara, who has three children, is an example. Like most parents, she worries about her children's health and safety. But, unlike most parents, her life is ruled almost entirely by her need to keep the children safe: she tries to arrange things so that risks are avoided as much as possible.

She takes the children everywhere by car so that they don't run into any dangers on the street. They aren't allowed to play with other children in case they catch an illness. They are shielded in every way from the dangers of the world.

The children, who are now reaching their teens, are beginning to resist and rebel and this worries Barbara even more. She doesn't realise that she is probably increasing the danger for her children, who will at some time have to make their own way in the world. She is also limiting her own world severely, placing all her hopes in the children – who will fly the nest eventually. It is her inability to cope with the natural anxieties of parenthood that is limiting her own and the children's freedom.

## Look for language

Some of the language devices we have already considered are useful if you are trying to help someone to overcome their fears. Watch out for ways in which they may be talking themselves into being more frightened than they need to be.

Supposing, for instance, you know that the person really does want to change but they say something like, 'I'm just not brave enough to say what I think. It's bound to cause a terrible row and I'll lose everything.' Encourage the person to think again. 'If you didn't have to worry about what would happen, what would you like to say?' or 'Supposing there is an argument, just what do you think you would lose?' or 'Is there a way of making a start without risking *everything*?' are all possible responses which could lead to a discussion and exploration.

Avoid implying that their fears are trivial or that the person is stupid for being scared – nothing turns people off more than this kind of criticism. Being willing to discuss the situation is more likely to give the message that you think the fears are important enough not to be ignored – but that they may not necessarily be a barrier.

## I just blew my top

Anger is another feeling which can stop us getting on with our lives. We get angry when we have been hurt unfairly – when we feel out of control of our world. Whereas fear tends to help us get out of a situation as quickly as possible, anger strengthens us so that we can confront the situation and fight it. Just like fear, anger is a natural response to a problem we are facing. Tension builds up, fuelling our body to face the threat to our control.

If the tension is released, we feel better – as you will know if you have ever shouted at someone and felt an immediate release of pressure. Unfortunately that feeling is often followed by embarrassment, guilt or some other negative emotion, as we realise that we have probably given ourselves an even greater problem than the one we were trying to solve!

Some of us find it hard to express anger. The reason may lie in the past: perhaps we grew up in a family where it wasn't very acceptable to express anger; or maybe being angry never seemed to solve the problem. For some people the feeling is too unpleasant; others are afraid that if they get angry they'll lose control, create a scene, embarrass themselves or hurt others. Whatever the reason, the anger is kept inside rather than discharged.

## Collecting stamps?

It's a mistake to think that anger will just go away if we ignore it. It can fester away inside, eroding our self-esteem. I once heard this compared to the way in which in the 1960s shops gave customers trading stamps with the goods they bought. For every pound you were given a stamp to stick in your book.

When you had saved up a certain amount you could cash in your collection for a gift. Some people preferred to save up the books until they could cash them in for a big prize; others cashed them in more frequently for small prizes.

Imagine that you could collect a stamp every time you felt angry and didn't outwardly express your feeling. You would stick the anger stamp in your psychological book; you might cash it in quite soon or, if you were a collector, save up your anger for years and then cash it in for a really big pay-off!

To outward appearances, for instance, Barbara is happy to make sacrifices to keep her children safe; but inwardly she is beginning to resent the way in which her own needs are being ignored. She is collecting stamps which one day she may cash in for the 'prize' of a speech in which she will blame the children or her partner for their lack of appreciation – or for an even greater 'prize' such as a divorce or a breakdown.

'Stamp collectors' often feel short-changed in life and tend to blame others for their problems because they feel they are not getting what they deserve. To change things, they would have to take more responsibility and work for what they want. Their reluctance to be direct in expressing how they feel and saying what they want means they are more likely to direct their anger outwards. Any passing slight adds to their collec-tion, which they either discharge constantly towards anyone and everyone who crosses their path or save up to cash in for a big scene every now and then.

## How to Help

The appropriate expression of anger is a necessary part of a healthy emotional life. There are two ways in which you might help someone who is being hurt by the anger they are feeling.

## Asking why

The first relates to when something has happened between you and someone you care about which causes either or both of you to feel angry. Even though it might lead to an uncomfortable exchange, it would be better for you both if you could talk about what had happened so that you can let the anger go.

If the other person is angry with you, encourage them to tell you why. 'Have I done something to upset you?' or 'I notice you've been cold towards me lately. Are you angry about something?' or 'I may have got this wrong, but I think I've done something you're cross about' are all possible ways of opening up the subject. All you have to do then is listen.

You may not feel particularly comfortable hearing someone's criticism of you, but once the matter is confronted openly and honestly the slate can be cleared. You can accept what truth there is in the other person's view; apologise for any problem you have caused; explore a bit further to try to find out where the problem lies or refute any misunderstanding which may have occurred – whatever is appropriate.

## Acknowledging anger

Sometimes people are so angry that they can only shout or sulk. If this is the case, you need to reduce the feelings of anger so that you can have a reasonable conversation about the problem. Probably the best way to do this is to acknowledge the anger rather than try to brush it off. 'I can see that you're very angry' is better than 'There's no need to be so angry.' It's difficult for someone to go on shouting once their anger has been recognised.

Then you can express your wish to understand and solve the problem; 'I want to hear what you have to say. Let's try and work this out together.' Let the person give voice to whatever is troubling them and use all your listening skills to try to understand where the problem lies. Don't move into justifying or explaining too soon; 'It sounds like this has been bothering you for some time'; 'This must have seemed like the last straw'; 'Is there anything else that is upsetting you?' are better than 'It's not my fault'; 'You're just as much to blame'; or 'Don't be so picky.'

Don't be afraid to admit the possibility that you have contributed to or caused the problem. 'Maybe I should have arrived earlier'; 'I did make a mistake'; 'It must have seemed to you that I didn't care' are better than 'I don't know what you mean'; 'I'm doing my best'; or 'It's nothing to do with me.'

## Use the Five Rs

If you are the angry one, you can use the tried and tested Five R formula first described in Chapter 5.

*Reflect* first, before you launch into confronting the person, on your motives for criticising them. Criticism can be used to coerce or punish someone, or for more constructive purposes like solving a problem or improving your relationship. If your main aim is that the other person should feel bad because of the way they have treated you, or you want to force them to change their behaviour, it's likely that you will achieve at best an uneasy truce and at worst a deepening conflict. You are much more likely to succeed if you have a genuine desire to improve the relationship between the two of you. If you decide to go ahead, the next thing you should do is . . .

*Report* what is happening. Be specific; talk about actions rather than the other person's character. Describe the behaviour which is upsetting you. 'You were an hour late yesterday' is better than 'You're so unreliable'; 'When you interrupt me . . .' is better than 'You never listen to me.' You can start off with a phrase like, 'I'd like to discuss something with you' or 'I've been worried about this for some time . . .'. Then . . .

*Relate* the effect of the behaviour on your thoughts and feelings. '. . . and I feel . . .', '. . . and I think . . .'. Concentrate on the effects of the actions rather than on your negative feelings. Say, for example, 'You were an hour late yesterday and I thought you'd forgotten our appointment. I felt let down'; 'When you interrupt me before I've finished what I want to say, I feel angry and frustrated. I think you don't consider my opinion important enough to hear.' This might be enough for you to begin a discussion with the other person. If not, the next stage is to ask them to behave differently. In which case . . .

*Request* in concrete terms whatever you need to be different. Make sure the request is reasonable and within the power of the other person to make it. For example, say, '. . . and I'd like you to let me know in future if you're delayed' or 'I'd like you to wait until I've finished what I've got to say before you tell me what you think.' If possible, end by talking about the . . .

*Result* you are hoping for. Say, for instance, '. . . because I'll be able to get on with something else while I'm waiting and I won't feel the time has been wasted' or '. . . because I won't end up feeling so frustrated'.

This might all sound rather long-winded, especially if you feel the event is not that important in itself. But remember, each stamp in itself has little value – it's when they are collected in numbers that they can be cashed in. The eventual 'prize' you might collect is a broken relationship because there are just too many wounds to heal. Difficulties are much more likely to occur when people try to modify their natural feelings to make them more acceptable to others.

The same kind of rules help if the person is angry about something with which you aren't involved. You can help by listening to them, letting them discharge some of their feelings and then discussing possible action. You might, for instance, encourage them to talk about their anger to the other party in the same way as we have just explored.

As a last point, there are times when it just isn't safe, appropriate or possible to advise speaking out your anger. There are other ways of letting it out which you can suggest. Imagine, for instance, that the person who has caused the offence is dressed in ridiculous clothes (or no clothes at all). It's amazing how anger can dissipate once you create a ridiculous image and have to laugh in spite of yourself. Writing a furious letter listing everything which is causing a problem is another way of dissipating angry. The letter is not meant to be posted but it can be put away and read in a little while. Making a phone call but keeping the button pressed down; putting a doll or a cushion on a chair and pretending it's the person who is causing the anger – in fact anything can work which allows imaginary contact within which feelings can be expressed in words. You can offer to role-play the offender so that your friend can practise confronting them.

In Chapter 10 we shall explore how we can help if feelings turn into depression.

# 10

# 'I'M REALLY DOWN IN
# THE DUMPS'

The previous chapter focused on the effect of feelings of anger and fear and how, if left unspoken, they could have a serious impact on the way we live. This chapter looks at ways in which we might support someone whose feelings have turned to depression.

Everyone feels sad from time to time, but when we talk of depression we are referring to something different and deeper. The term covers a broad spectrum from a passing feeling of 'the blues' to a severe psychotic state. It is well known that many famous high-achieving people suffered from depression, among them Winston Churchill, Abraham Lincoln, Sigmund Freud and Evelyn Waugh, whose novel *The Ordeal of Gilbert Pinfold* is based on his own depressive experience.

## *What Is It?*

It is still not really known what causes depression. Clinically speaking, it would appear to be some malfunction of chemicals, called neurotransmitters, which carry between the millions of brain cells the electrical impulses which are eventually translated into thoughts and actions by the body. Some of the drugs used in the treatment of depression are known to affect these neurotransmitters. Deficiencies of certain vitamins have also been implicated.

We do know, though, that people get depressed for all sorts of reasons. The condition can be triggered by the kind of crises we have explored in previous chapters, such as the death of a loved one, the break-up of a marriage or partnership, or being made redundant. It would, of course, be surprising if people didn't react to such situations with emotions that were permeated with sadness, feelings of helplessness and a dwindling sense of self-value. In the natural course of events, these feelings pass as the person comes to terms with the situation and moves into the future.

Sometimes, though, the person cannot extricate themselves from those feelings. They become inactive and apathetic, abandoning their usual interests and hobbies, and not bothering to take care with their appearance and personal hygiene. They may appear agitated and be constantly on the move, but achieve little. Sufferers tend to wake very early in the morning and lie in bed worrying about their perceived failures and inadequacies. There can be other physical consequences. Loss of appetite, weight loss, constipation, headaches, back-ache and stomach cramps are all symptoms which can add to the person's distress, not least because they seem inexplicable. At the other end of the scale, some people swing from a state of depression to one of over-activity, becoming uninhibited and extravagant in their behaviour. These swings from euphoria to depression are distressing and difficult.

Depression is not a trivial matter. At the severe end of the spectrum people experience extreme feelings of guilt or shame about imagined or minor faults which can be overwhelming; they see themselves to blame for everything which has gone wrong. At its most extreme, depression can lead to serious self-neglect or even suicide.

> '*I felt as if I was in a grey world – I felt numb as if I was grey inside. There was no colour at all. There seemed no point in trying to do anything; there was no point to anything. I can't even say I felt sad – I just felt nothing. I would listen to people speaking and I would hear myself reply, but I couldn't tell you a minute later what we had been talking about. Nothing registered. Sometimes it didn't even seem worth getting out of bed.*'
>
> Eleanor

> '*I was seeing a therapist who suggested I drew a picture to show how I felt. I drew a cage with enormous bars criss-crossing the whole page. I put myself right in the corner of the cage – a tiny figure with bowed head and drooping shoulders, a prisoner. There was no way I could get out of the prison. It was like I was being held down by some invisible force, and yet I knew that I only had to open the door and I could go free. In my drawing, though, I notice I didn't put any door.*'
>
> John

No one is immune from depression. Sometimes it just seems to happen out of the blue, or it can follow a loss or accumulation of losses. It can be exacerbated by debilitation due to illness or disability, or by poor social circumstances. A lack of close personal relationships can lower the spirits and be a contributing factor – and this, of course, is where you could come in.

## *What You Can Do To Help*

Supporting someone who is depressed isn't easy. In cases of severe depression it is well-nigh impossible, because the person really needs professional help of some kind – either drugs or psychotherapy. Even when the depression isn't severe enough to warrant treatment, it can be hard to spend time with someone for whom the smallest thing is too much to cope with.

It's easy to lose patience and tell the person to pull themselves together, look on the bright side, count their blessings and so on. It's silly and unkind, though, to tell depressed people to take responsibility for themselves. It's a bit like telling someone who has broken their leg to throw away their crutch and walk properly. If they were able to 'pull themselves together' they wouldn't be in this state in the first place.

### Take avoiding action

If you know someone well enough, you might be able to help head off a depression which you think might arise in the near future. For instance, people who retire from work are often unprepared for how low they can feel after the first novelty has worn off. They might have been looking forward to the event for a long time but overlooked the losses – a purposeful job, status, companionship, structure to the day and so on.

Sometimes people who have made an important decision like moving house, changing their job or buying a new car become depressed. They keep asking themselves if they could have made a better choice. They begin to regret the way they have committed themselves. In a sense there is a loss here, too. The loss is that of the freedom of making any choice.

All the time you don't make up your mind, the possibilities remain for you to do anything. Once you have decided, you have lost the opportunity of the other options.

Most people agree that action is the antithesis to depression. If you are involved with someone who you suspect might become low as the result of an impending event, you could help by making a point of discussing the future and deciding upon plans of action. People who have prepared for retirement, for instance, are less likely to become depressed; moving into the course of action that a decision requires gives little space for regrets.

## Talk, talk, talk!

We have already explored in some depth the value of allowing someone to talk about their feelings. Now let's look at the way unexpressed feelings can contribute to depression.

Imagine for a moment that you have just experienced a hurt or loss and feel pain as a result. There are three kinds of loss which cause most hurt: the loss of someone you love, the loss of control, and the loss of self-esteem. The pain you feel creates energy inside you which needs to be directed outward at the source of the pain. Let's call this energy anger.

There may be many reasons why you cannot express this anger outwardly – maybe you would risk losing your job, your partner or your reputation. Maybe you are afraid you will be overtaken by the anger and won't be able to control yourself, or that the other person will retaliate. Whether your fears are reasonable or not, they prevent you from expressing your feelings.

However, the anger doesn't just disappear; if it can't be discharged outwards, it will turn inwards against yourself. The anger might then change to other feelings like guilt or shame, which inevitably lead to feelings of unworthiness and inadequacy.

At this point you could relieve the guilt by accepting the original anger as a reasonable response to the original hurt. If you don't, the feelings deepen and become depression, which then consumes energy. It's a vicious circle: pain of loss leads to anger which, if held in, leads to guilt which, if unrelieved, leads to depression.

Talking about, or being allowed to talk about, these feelings will not, of course, solve the original problem. But it will help avoid the depression which can occur if the feelings are kept down or 'depressed'. Aim to encourage the person to lift themselves out of the swamp of feelings in which they may have immersed themselves so that they can move more freely. They will be able to use this freed energy to make decisions and take action which could improve matters.

## Listen and share

A relationship in which you can both listen and share has great therapeutic potential. It means sharing your own weaknesses and concerns and accepting the other person's distress without pushing it away. Saying things like 'It can't be as bad as that' or 'Don't worry, it'll all turn out all right' has the effect of belittling the other person's experience. It leaves them feeling even worse because they feel they are not worth listening to. You may find you have nothing very much to say, but a comforting hug or a hand on the shoulder can carry the message you want to convey.

## Don't play the game

The American psychologist, Eric Berne, identified repetitive patterns of behaviour which he called 'Games'. He believed that each of us has a range of unconscious psychological and emotional needs, the need for acceptance or attention for instance, which we attempt to meet in our everyday life. If, as we develop through our childhood, we cannot meet these needs satisfactorily, we develop ways of behaving to compensate. These behaviours become so habitual that we are not conscious of them. The problem is that because the needs are out of our everyday awareness, we can't just acknowledge them and ask for them to be met. We have developed ways of behaving which we hope will solve the problem. Psychological games always have a hidden agenda. What is going on on the surface is not what the communication is truly about. They seem to follow a pattern with a predictable outcome.

If you have ever found yourself in a situation which feels familiar but ends up with you and whoever else is involved feeling bad, you were probably engaged in a psychological game. You find yourself thinking thoughts like, 'Oh, no! Not again!' or 'Why did I let that happen again?' or 'Why does this keep on happening to me?'

One game which people who are depressed often play is what Eric Berne called 'Why Don't You . . . Yes, but . . .'. It goes like this:

*Depressed person:* 'I feel so low. I'm so tired; life is so dreary.'

*Helpful friend:* 'Why don't you take a break; what you really need is a good holiday.'

*Depressed person:* 'Yes, but I could never get time off from work'

*Helpful friend:* 'Oh! Why don't you arrange to go away for a weekend. Then you wouldn't have to take time off.'

*Depressed person:* 'Yes, but I wouldn't enjoy being by myself in a hotel.'

*Helpful friend:* 'Why don't you find someone to go with you?'

*Depressed person:* 'Yes, I could do that, but I hate sharing a room and it's expensive to go as a single person. And anyway I'm so behind with work that I ought to work at the weekend.'

And so it goes on until one or the other (probably the helpful friend) gets tired of the conversation.

Playing the role of the helpful friend dooms you to feelings of frustration and helplessness, so avoid playing this game if you can. If you find yourself in this kind of communication you can be fairly certain that the other person has, for some reason or other, more interest in resisting help than in accepting it.

It's possible that the advice you are offering is unacceptable and they just want to reject it politely. Or it may be that there is a deeper psychological dynamic which prevents them allowing themselves to be helped. Either way it will come to an unsatisfactory close for both of you.

If you find the words 'Why don't you . . .' hovering on your lips, find something else to say. Try, for instance, 'What would you like to be doing?'; 'It's hard to get up energy when you're feeling down', or even 'I'm not going to make any suggestions because you always find a "Yes, but . . ."'!

## Invite selfishness

It may seem odd to suggest that you might encourage the other person to be more selfish. Very often depressed people strike us as self-obsessed because they tend to experience the world only through their own perceptions and needs, which means they are out of touch with the needs of others. On the other hand, people who are depressed are not very good at looking after themselves. Depression is a very punishing experience for both body and mind. The person who is depressed will often treat themselves badly: instead of resting they will struggle to work; when they do have time to relax and think pleasant thoughts, they tend to engage in negative thinking, always imagining the worst; rather than eat regular nourishing and tasty food, they tend to snack on junk food or go without.

If you were looking after someone who was physically ill, it would seem perfectly reasonable to encourage them to nurture themselves – and they would probably accept that as a sensible thing to do. However, because lack of self-esteem is so much a part of depression it becomes hard for the depressed person to be kind to themselves.

Inviting someone for a walk in the country; preparing a nutritious, tasty meal; presenting them with a jar of luxurious body cream; or offering a massage are all examples of things you might do to encourage a little selfishness. None of them will magically dissolve the depression, but each of them might give the person a glimpse of light in the greyness of their world. Finding something active to do is nearly always more rewarding than trying to give advice.

> '*I hated it when people said things like, "You'll feel better soon. Time is a great healer" or "You've got to make an effort." I thought they were probably right, but it just made things worse. The best thing I remember from that time is when my friend Sarah came round one day and told me we were going out. If she'd asked me I'd have said I didn't feel like it, but she didn't give me any opportunity to argue. "Just*

get in the car," she said, so I did – it was easier than arguing. We drove to the country. We didn't talk much but I suddenly got a sense of the world outside myself. I can't really describe it – it was as if a window opened and I could breathe more easily. I wasn't great company that day, but Sarah didn't seem to mind. She was also enjoying being out of the city. It was a lovely gesture – just the right thing to do at the time.

Eleanor

## Helping someone to help themselves

There are definitely certain actions which stand a good chance of reducing someone's depression. Your problem as the helper is that, although you may know what these actions are, you cannot perform them for the person – they have to take the action themselves. If the person you are trying to help really wants to improve their condition there are several avenues you can try, but if they don't you may just have to stand by and give whatever support you can.

'Being depressed was just like being in a swamp. The more I struggled to get out the deeper I was drawn into it. I wanted to be pulled out, but whenever someone tried to help I couldn't respond. I think it was a bit like when I was learning to swim. The more I splashed around the harder it was – but I had to keep splashing to keep my head above water. At some point I must have realised that it was easier to swim if I stopped trying so hard – but that needed so much confidence. When I was down, I just couldn't trust myself – or anyone else – to save me.'

John

## Don't tell me to relax – it's only my stress that's keeping me together!

When someone is depressed it's very hard for them to relax. Their great fear is that if they stop struggling things will get even worse and they will become even less able to cope. This makes it very hard for the person trying to help. If you have ever taught someone to swim you will know that it is the moment they stop fighting the water and trust themselves that they begin to swim properly. You will also know that telling the would-be water-baby to 'relax and let the water hold you up' is not at all helpful – they believe they will drown if they do so. Similarly, there's not much point in telling a depressed person to relax and be peaceful; they believe their tension is holding them together, and that to let go means falling apart.

However, many therapists who work with depressed people are agreed that the ability to relax physically does play a part in relieving the mind of its tension. Dorothy Rowe, a clinical psychologist who has written many books on the subject, calls this 'finding a peaceful place within yourself'. Learning to relax physically will stand a person in good stead whenever they feel over-stressed; learning to relax mentally is even more helpful, especially since depression carries such a pattern of negative thinking.

Perhaps you can persuade the person you are helping to have some lessons with a teacher of relaxation or meditation – yoga or Tai-Chi, for example. If you have never tried out these ideas yourself, you could start together – you, too, would experience the benefits.

### Stepping out

Something else which you could bear in mind is that recent research studies have shown that exercise can have advantageous effects on depression. For instance, in an experiment carried out by McCann and Holmes in 1984 a group of very depressed women were split into three groups; one group were assigned to a regular aerobic exercise class, the second were taught muscle relaxation and instructed to practise it daily, while the third had no treatment of this kind. The group in the exercise class showed the greatest reduction in depression. So if you can encourage the person whom you are helping to take regular aerobic exercise, their depression may improve.

## Finding a counsellor

Many people nowadays are helped to sort out their unhappiness by going to a counsellor or therapist. A well-trained, professional counsellor will be able to help your friend or relative differently and perhaps more deeply than you can. They have no vested interest in maintaining a personal relationship; their only aim is to help their client live more resourcefully and satisfyingly. A good counsellor will help their client understand themselves and the choices they have before them.

You can help by encouraging the person to choose a counsellor with care. They can ask at the first session about the arrangements for sessions, the way fees are worked out, and whether there are cancellation charges; they can ask about the professional qualifications of the therapist and what particular theory underpins their practice. If these kind of questions aren't answered directly, it would be a good idea to look for another therapist.

You might also be able to help the person keep up their motivation. There are bound to be times during the counselling process when painful experiences are brought into the memory, or when it isn't at all clear how continuing with the sessions will improve things. Sometimes it feels as if the counselling is making things worse, because feelings which have been kept down for so long are emerging. You need to reassure the person that this is to be expected and that, providing he or she has trust in the counsellor, it really is worth going on.

Many people are also apprehensive about seeking counselling or therapy because they think that others will see them as weak, ill or crazy. They believe they will go down in people's estimation. You can prove them wrong by supporting and expressing your approval of their decision.

## It's not easy

You will already know that trying to help someone who is depressed is not at all easy. However, there are some things you may be able to do to make things a little or a great deal better for the person. It is important, though, that you avoid getting sucked into the feelings of hopelessness and helplessness that depressed people can project. Remember that each person, in the end, is responsible for the way they choose to respond to life. There will always be some people who see the glass as half-full and others who see it as half-empty. Don't let your own view of life be dimmed by whoever you are trying to help.

# 11

# 'THE DOCTOR SAID . . .'

How can you find the right words when you hear that someone you care about has become seriously or even terminally
ill? You obviously want to be positive, but at the same time,
you don't want to be seen as a 'Pollyanna'. (As it happens,
Pollyanna has got a bad name – but as I remember, she was a
girl who saw everything in its best light and in the end
persuaded everyone else to do so too. Is that such a bad thing?)
Be that as it may, it can be very wearing to be with someone
who refuses to acknowledge the darker side of life. On the
other hand, you need to be able to talk about what is happening without sinking into a despairing mood.

## *Make It Possible To Talk*

When people discover they are seriously ill, one of the difficult
things for them is to know how to talk about it to others. Some

don't talk about it at all, others choose a few very close people to share the news with, yet others talk about it to everyone. Iris, for instance, chose to write this letter:

> '*I am writing to all my friends because I want you all to know about what is happening to me, and it is easier for me to write than to tell each one of you separately. My cancer has returned and I don't think I will survive this bout. I am fortunate to have a consultant who is very supportive, empathic and direct – she has suggested that I have maybe six months, perhaps more but no guarantee.*
>
> '*I want you to know that, although I will fight this as much as I can, I don't want this time to be totally focused around my illness. I want to live as fully as possible – there are lots of things I want to do. I want our contact to be as it always has; I am willing to talk about my situation, but I want to know about yours too. I expect if I get really ill I will also get self-obsessed, but I don't feel that way now. I can't say I'm not nervous – but I don't feel terrified! I don't believe in an after-life but I do feel that I am part of the life cycle – to be born, to grow and to die is the natural way. I want to hold on to this idea as much as I can.*
>
> '*I realise this news may give you pain, which I know is a mark of our closeness – but please don't be so upset that you can't face me. To lose contact with my friends would be more painful to me than the cancer! So phone, fax, write, call round . . . soon.*
>
>        *All my love,*
>        *Iris.*'

When the first shock and distress had passed, her friends came to appreciate this letter a great deal, because it gave them clues as to how to behave in the face of this distressing news.

So perhaps the first – and most important – point to make is that you mustn't let your own distress and awkwardness prevent you from staying in contact with a friend or relative who is ill. A good friend would rather you be awkward and present than comfortable and absent.

If you are unsure whether to talk about the illness or not, ask the person what they would prefer. A simple question like 'Do you want to talk about it?' will do. Your friend or relative might be sick and tired of talking about it or desperate to exchange ideas and describe their feelings about it. Either way, try to make it easy for them to do what they want.

Something else to consider is whether you share your reactions with the person involved. It's probably more constructive to say, at least briefly, how you are feeling. If you don't, you are likely to find it difficult to have an authentic conversation of any depth because you will be hiding your own powerful feelings. You don't have to dwell on misery and sadness, but you will find that once you have spoken about your thoughts and feelings you won't have to use up energy to keep them down. Once again, keep it simple. 'I was so unhappy to hear . . .'; 'It came as a shock to us . . .'; 'We are all so sorry . . .'.

## *Beware The Rescuer*

As in most of the other situations we have explored, what you do is just as important as what you say. Before you launch into helping, find out what the other person would find most useful. When someone we love is ill, there is a temptation to take over everything – but you need to be careful about becoming too much of a 'rescuer'.

In the world of counselling, 'rescuing' is not, generally speaking, thought to be a good thing. A rescuer sees someone such as a sick person as being less able than themselves, and therefore discounts that person's ability to think and act on their own initiative. So a rescuer is a person who is always very helpful but often does things for which people haven't actually asked; someone who often does more than their fair share or things which they really don't *want* to do but feel they *ought* to do.

Admittedly, on the surface there seems to be nothing wrong with this. Helping someone who is weaker, younger or more inexperienced than ourselves is a good thing to do. Putting someone else's needs above our own because we feel we have a duty is commendable.

The problem arises when, in a relationship, one person always acts as the rescuer. This can have the effect of making the other person feel more helpless than they actually are. Every time you perform a task for someone which they could do for themselves, the underlying message is, 'I'm doing this for you because I don't trust you to do it for yourself.' The other person either colludes and may actually come to believe that they are helpless, or gets resentful and fights off the help. This, in turn, causes the rescuer to feel hurt and misunderstood. In any case, communication between the two people becomes inauthentic; neither can really say what they feel for fear of how the other might respond.

This is Hannah, now seriously disabled as a result of MS, talking about her mother who lives nearby:

> '*I get so mad with my mother. She arrives most days and busies herself around the house. She wouldn't think of phoning to see if I wanted her to come; sometimes I'm really*

*grateful because she does things which I find too difficult. But I'm getting to resent her being so busy.*

*'She makes me coffee – you'd think by now she would know that I don't like coffee! But in she comes with the little tray beautifully arranged with biscuits, sometimes a flower in a vase, lovely – and the coffee (ugh!) The trouble is that she's so obviously trying to help that I can't tell her that sometimes I need to muddle through on my own, so that I can prove to myself that I can still do something useful.*

*'I also hate the way that she – mark you, she's not the only one – assumes that, because I'm so physically disabled now, my mind has also gone. I'd like to be asked whether I want something or not. But how can I say anything? She'd be hurt, and things would be worse between us.'*

The simplest way to avoid rescuing is to ask what's wanted. 'How can I help?'; 'Would you like me to . . .?' 'What would you like me to do?' By checking in this kind of way, you are also sending the other person the message: 'You have the right to make decisions about yourself, and I trust you to take responsibility.'

Make sure you aren't offering more than you can actually deliver. It can feel good to commit yourself to helping, but it can also become a burden if you over-commit yourself. If that happens, at best you will begin to feel resentful, and at worst you will start letting the other person down. Sometimes it's possible to work together with a group of friends or relatives to share whatever help is required rather than to take it all on yourself. It may not feel so saintly, but it might be more practical!

# *Be A Welcome Visitor*

There are no rules which would make our visits to someone who is seriously ill or dying as positive an experience as possible for everyone concerned. You will need to be guided by your knowledge of the person to decide what they would find most comforting. Here are some ideas which could help.

## Listen first, talk later

We have returned to the importance of listening time and time again in this book. It's just as important for someone who is sick or dying to be listened to with care and understanding.

## It's sometimes enough just to be present

There may be times when the person you are visiting doesn't want to talk, but also does not want to be alone. You can sit together, perhaps holding hands. You don't need to find words to fill in the silences; over and over again people have said that the clichés which others use when they are feeling uncomfortable are meaningless to them.

## Know when to go

Comforting though it usually is to have visitors when you are ill, it can also be extremely tiring. Be as sensitive as you can to matching the length of your visit to the energy of the sick person.

## Recognise symbols

In their book *On Becoming a Counsellor*, Eugene Kennedy and Sara Charles make the point that dying people often speak symbolically. They may tell a story, recount a particular memory or make a gesture. If we are aware that the person may be wanting to get across an important message, we may be able to catch their meaning and give words to what they are only able to outline in symbols.

A mother might, for instance, pick up and caress a photograph of her children, wanting them to know how much she loves them; an ex-soldier might ask to see his wartime medals, needing to communicate his remembered grief at the loss of comrades; a wife might tell of the time she first met her husband, eager for him to know how important he was to her.

### I'm still here

It's easy to treat someone who is seriously ill as if they were not really there. It's similar to the way disabled people are often ignored as people talk to their carer – the 'Does she take sugar?' scenario! People can forget how much seriously ill people can hear and understand. Talking *about* someone rather than *to* them diminishes the sense of self, which is so important.

## *It Helps To Know What's Happening*

We have seen before how, when people are faced with a crisis, they tend to follow a predictable path. Dr Elizabeth Kubler-Ross has written extensively on her observations and research on the experience of dying patients. She observes that, as people come to terms with death, they pass through similar stages to the way we face other crises in our lives.

Having some awareness of this may well help you understand what is happening with your friend or relative, although other writers have observed that stages vary considerably from person to person. It is useful to have a theory as a guide because it helps you put things into some kind of order, but you can't make people fit a theory. As always, your main guide will be the person themselves – they will give you the best guidance of all.

Dr Kubler-Ross first mentions denial. The person makes some effort to carry on as usual, going perhaps from doctor to doctor trying to disprove the diagnosis and even avoiding telling the family the truth of the situation.

The next stage is that of anger and questioning: 'Why me?' Sometimes the person's anger spills over on whoever is present, so should that happen to be you don't take it personally.

Dr Kubler-Ross then talks about a stage of 'bargaining'. It's as if the person is trying to put off the day of reckoning with all sorts of resolutions to do with reform and better behaviour.

As the person grows to realise that death is really coming, depression may follow as they become acutely aware of losses in the past and the potential loss in the future. As the illness progresses, the person begins slowly to withdraw their interest from the world outside them. The circle of those in whom interest is shown becomes smaller and smaller.

## *Iris's Story*

Earlier in this chapter we read the letter from Iris, telling of the return of her cancer eight years after the removal of the original tumour. She was determined to live to the full and, using a combination of orthodox and complementary medicine, enjoyed life for two more years. She travelled, gave dinner parties, visited her children and grandchildren, and spent time with her friends. During that time she talked about death quite openly. There were discussions about near-death experiences which various people had had; about how comforting it would be to have a strong religious belief; about what might happen in the world at large; about how the grandchildren were likely to turn out, and so on. Kubler-Ross's psychological stages were analysed; sometimes Iris could identify with them, sometimes not.

Iris made it easy for those around her because she was clear about the reality of her illness and its prognosis. She was willing to talk about it, but not obsessed with it. She was determined to get on with her life. Her view was that she was much more comfortable with people who knew and who could talk about what was happening to her. Sometimes, inevitably, she or her friends would get upset and have a weep together, but that was acceptable and there were as many laughs and good times as there were sad moments.

She died, as she wished, at home. She was cared for by a specialist nurse and members of her family and friends. She had, together with those she loved, planned her memorial service, and the music and poetry of that occasion are our lasting memory. She included this piece by Henry Scott Holland:

*Death is nothing at all; I have only slipped away into the next room. I am I and you are you. Whatever we were to each other, that we are still. Call me by my old familiar name, speak to me in the easy way which you always used. Put no difference into your tone; wear no forced air of solemnity or sorrow. Laugh as we always laughed at the little jokes we enjoyed together. Play, smile, think of me, pray for me. Let my name be ever the household word that it always was. Let it be spoken without effect, without the ghost of a shadow on it. Life means all that it ever meant. It is the same as it ever was; there is absolutely unbroken continuity. What is this death but a negligible accident? Why should I be out of mind because I am out of sight? I am but waiting for you, for an interval, somewhere very near, just around the corner. All is well.*

# 12

# WHAT ARE FRIENDS FOR?

So far, of course, the focus of this book has been on the person you are helping: what they may be thinking and feeling, and what you can do to make things easier for them. In this last chapter let's put the spotlight on you. Most of us like to think of ourselves as helpful people, and for much of the time helping is an instinctive action. We see someone about to slip over and we put an arm out to save them; someone drops their shopping and we help them pick things up; someone's car has broken down so we stop to see if we can help. These are simple acts of kindness which also satisfy our own need to be of use. In this book we have been exploring the deeper kind of helping which occurs when we are committed to trying to make a difference for someone we care about.

This kind of helping requires us to give of ourselves. The more deeply we care about someone, the more their predicament creates strong feelings in us. The person may be someone at the centre of our lives whose situation affects us directly in many different ways. It may be someone whom we have known for a very long time and with whom many experiences have been shared. It could be someone whom we have grown to love and respect for the qualities they bring to the relationship. It is likely that we want things to go well for the person, for them to be successful, health and happy. It is possible that we could have experienced a similar situation to the one they are in, and as a result painful memories are raised. On the other hand we may be in uncharted waters, facing a situation about which we have no experience at all. Either way, our efforts to help will take up energy and can leave us confused and tired.

## *Look After Yourself*

This may be a strange idea for a book which is essentially about looking after other people. However, just because looking after others isn't always easy it's an important consideration. One way to look after yourself is to be very clear about your motives for wanting to help. There are a few questions you can ask yourself to help you become clearer:

### Why do I want to do it?

Helping others is not a totally unselfish act. Our behaviour is largely governed by the necessity to fulfil those psychological needs of which we are usually unaware but which have developed as an essential part of our personality. They are very basic and include our need to be accepted and loved; to be in control of our world; and to be safe. How we go about fulfilling them depends on the particular sense we made of the world as we first became aware of our existence in it; those early 'decisions' tend to influence us right into our adult life.

For instance, we might have developed the notion that in order to be accepted we must please everyone around us by sacrificing our own needs to look after theirs. By helping people, we will be seen as 'good' and so people will love us. Subscribing to this belief makes helping part of a deal – which, of course, the other person doesn't know about. Things are fine as long as we are getting the 'reward' of feeling accepted, but if for some reason the reward is not forthcoming or is not enough we will end up with uncomfortable feelings such as depression, resentment and being unappreciated.

Another scenario is one based on the idea that by helping others we are able to confirm that we ourselves are OK. Being with someone who is apparently not managing their life very well can make us feel better about how we are managing our own; someone who is less fortunate than ourselves can make our own problems seem less important. It's a bit like becoming a marriage guidance counsellor because your own marriage isn't so good. The problem here is that sooner or later we realise that our own situation hasn't really changed, and so the whole thing becomes a burden.

There is an argument that it doesn't really matter *why* one person helps another, as long as they do. When there is an emergency or when the help is of a short-term and superficial nature, that is probably true. It's more problematic, though, when we become involved at a deeper level. The best position from which to help someone is from a feeling of freedom of choice. We can choose to help because we want life to be better for another person, not because we want to bolster an idea of our own 'goodness', or to gain intimacy, a sense of purpose or usefulness. We are not so much helping out from the point of view of 'me' needing to look after 'you', but because it's 'us'.

## What can I do?

Something else to be clear about is what you can offer at this particular time. Your resources of energy, time, knowledge, patience and so on aren't limitless. Take a moment to think about what is going to be reasonable for you, and make that clear to the other person. Take your other commitments into consideration – there is no point in helping one person at the expense of an agreement you have with someone else, unless you are able to renegotiate that arrangement. For example, you can spend time with your seriously ill neighbour *provided* you can negotiate with your partner for them to spend more time looking after your children. The person you are helping may be slightly taken aback by your clarity, especially if they are not used to it. But they are much more likely to appreciate limited but reliable help from you than promises which just cannot be kept.

## How can I help?

Be clear, also, about what resources, skills or knowledge you have that might be of practical use. The first part of this book, for instance, was about the skills of communication. You will have your own particular store of information, insight and practical abilities to offer too. If you haven't got what is needed, you may know who has, so you might recommend or refer. Your judgement about what is useful to offer and when to offer it is important. Sometimes you may judge that it would be more helpful to allow the person to manage themselves than for you to rush in and take over.

# *Know How To Manage Your Pain*

For me, the definition of love is the quality of connection between people which means that each is affected by the other. If one is happy, so is the other; if one is sad, the other feels the sadness; if one is in pain, the other also feels it. So it is fairly inevitable that being with someone you care for means you will experience strong emotions yourself. You cannot blame them or hold them responsible; these feelings are *your* response to what is happening. Try to stay aware of how you are feeling and develop your own way of managing these emotions, so that they don't drag you down or cause you so much stress that you get ill.

There are many possible ways of relieving your mind and body, for instance; meditating, exercise, reading, playing, walking, gardening, going to a film, having a bath, taking time on your own. This list may seem like condoning self-indulgence, but if you are involved in supporting someone going through a difficult time you will need to keep up your strength and energy so that you can give the best possible help.

## *Who Cares For The Carer?*

To sum up, finding the right words and actions with which to help someone in trouble isn't as easy as it might seem. Taking care of yourself means you will be able to take care of others better. Part of taking care of yourself is knowing others who can take care of you when necessary. It's great to know that you have a network of people on whom you can call if you need.

In the past, people tended to live in much closer proximity to each other than most of us do now. When they were in trouble, there was always someone around who knew and who could help out. The disadvantage would have been the lack of privacy. These days many of us live quite isolated lives, either alone or in our small nuclear family. We treasure our privacy, but pay the price by not having a natural community of which we are part.

However, we are not programmed to live in solitude; we have evolved as social beings. Most people, if they were asked, 'What kind of world do you want to live in?', would probably include in their reply something like words along these lines: 'I'd like to know for certain that people cared about me, and I'd like them to know that I cared about them.' The more you find the words to say and the actions that go with them, the sooner that world will come about.

# REFERENCES AND FURTHER READING

ALEXANDER, Laurel, *Surviving Redundancy*, How To Books, 1996

CHRISTIE, Margaret J. and Mellet, Peter G. (eds), *The Psychosomatic Approach: Contemporary Practice of Whole-Person Care*, John Wiley & Sons, 1986

DAINOW, Sheila, *Be Your Own Counsellor*, Piatkus, 1997

EGAN, Gerard, *The Skilled Helper*, Brooks/Cole Publishing Co., 1982

HORWOOD, Janet, *Comfort for Depression*, Sheldon Press, 1982

KELLEY, Patricia, *Companion to Grief*, Piatkus, 1997

KUBLER-ROSS, Elizabeth, *On Death and Dying*, Routledge, 1969

KUPFERMANN, Jeannette, *When the Crying's Done*, Robson Books, 1992

LEVER, Dr Ruth, *A Guide to Common Illnesses*, Penguin, 1990

LOVELL, Anne, *Out of Work – A Family Affair*, Sheldon Press, 1996

MARRIS, Peter, *Loss and Change*, Routledge and Kegan Paul, 1978

MOONEY, Bel, *Perspectives for Living: Conversations on Bereavement and Love*, John Murray, 1992

MURRAY PARKES, Colin, *Bereavement*, Penguin, 1975

ROWE, Dorothy, *Depression*, Routledge and Kegan Paul, 1983

SERAGANIAN, Peter (ed), *Exercise Psychology: the Influence of Physical Exercise on Psychological Processes*, John Wiley & Sons, 1993

STEWART, Ian and Joines, Vann, *TA Today: A New Introduction to Transactional Analysis*, Lifespace Publishing, 1987

# INDEX

**Also available from Piatkus Books
by the same author**

# BE YOUR OWN COUNSELLOR

### A STEP-BY-STEP
### GUIDE TO
### UNDERSTANDING
### YOURSELF BETTER

## SHEILA DAINOW

**0 7499 1586 2    Pb    176pp   £8.99**

*Be Your Own Counsellor* is a unique book which explores
the idea of counselling yourself at home. Sheila Dainow
takes you step by step through the various stages of the
counselling process. Each chapter mirrors a professional
counselling session, and in working through the special
questions and exercises you will be using typical counselling methods to explore yourself and your life.

This practical and reassuring book will help you develop
a better understanding of yourself. You will find it easier
to make decisions, take more control over the way in
which you respond to difficult situations and view your
problems from a different perspective. You will have the
confidence and ability to make changes to your life.